MW00425413

Writing Your Novel
Using the Bible as Your Guide

A Writer For Life

The works of fiction and non-fiction mentioned in this book
are for reference only. The author does not affiliate with or
promote any titles. All Scriptures referenced are from the King
James Version

Text copyright © 2016 Jaimie Engle
Cover design © 2016 Jaimie Engle
Edited by A Writer For Life
The text for this book is set in Fairfield
All rights reserved, including the right of reproduction
in whole or in part in any form.

Published in the United States by A Writer For Life, LLC,
Melbourne, FL 32935.

To hire marketing, coaching, or editing services,
visit us on the Web: awriterforlife.com
A Writer For Life, the Coach For Your Dreams

ISBN-10: 0-9971709-6-4
ISBN-13: 978-0-9971709-6-2

10 9 8 7 6 5 4 3 2

I dedicate this book to students.
May it provide a new way to study the Bible and
new technique for writers to emulate.

Tribecca,
Keep writing!
SME
2017

WRITING YOUR NOVEL

USING THE BIBLE AS YOUR GUIDE

BOOK ONE

A Writer For Life Sell More Books Series

Introduction

God knows how to write. His associations include, the Author of Creation and the Beginning and the End. He wrote the Book of Life and the Bible, notably a worldwide best-seller translated into over 500 languages (www.wycliffe.net). Just to compare, *Harry Potter* by J.K. Rowling has been translated into seventy languages. (www.harrypotter.wikia.com) There was the time God wrote on the wall at a wedding (Daniel 5). And the time Jesus wrote in the sand and saved an adulteress (John 8). He wrote the Law on tablets for Moses—two drafts because Moses broke the first edition—and He's written His words on our hearts. God is the master author. So why wouldn't we want to study under Him?

This guide will breakdown Bible stories into their key story elements. It will show basic writing techniques such as character, plot, foreshadow, symbolism, metaphor & simile, setting, theme, and over arcing story line between the chapters. It will also serve as a comprehensive, though not exhaustive, Bible study. As an author who loves God and the Bible, this book states my own observations and connections in an effort to grow in God's word while growing as a writer.

Table of Contents

Chapter One:

In the Beginning

"In the beginning, God created the Heavens and the Earth."

Talk about great first lines! From page one we jump right into the Creation story. Why? Because our planet, our universe, is the setting for every page of the Bible from Genesis to Revelation; the story of a God who created the perfect place and populated it with amazing creatures and two main characters, a world where they could build a relationship with their Father. But the children misbehaved when an antagonist brought conflict into the story world, and God was forced to banish his beloved before they ate fruit of the tree that would cause Evil to gain control of the realm forever.

Man, I just thought of dozens of storylines that fit that mold. *Pinocchio. Legend. Lord of the Rings. Percy Jackson.* This is a great plot line to work with, and it really is the string that connects the Bible into a single book. God's people are constantly misbehaving and following Evil things leading them away from God. Until a hero rises from the dust to face an impending army of darkness, rescue the beloved, and save the day. Ultimately, this hero is seen in Christ on the cross, and that's where the story shifts.

The New Testament stories are not the same as the Old Testament ones. No longer do we see the conflicted people sin and repent; sin and repent. Now, the story focuses on the group whose mission is to spread God's Word at all costs; do the right thing even unto death. *Robin Hood. The Matrix. X-Men.* Sure, bad things are still happening in the world, but the hero's plight has changed.

The ultimate end is the Return of the Messiah and the defeat of darkness in Revelation. But like any good book, that's not the real ending. After 1,000 years, the Darkness will again be released for a time until Satan and his horde are cast into the Lake of Fire. The End.

The Bible on a whole has a clear beginning, middle, and end. Creation—Salvation—Rebirth. The theme throughout is the Redemption story; the sacrifice and saving of the undeserving "us." It's a beautiful illustration that tugs on our heartstrings and moves us emotionally when we see the concept in literature and movies. Why? Because it's built into us to need a savior; to know we are helpless and powerless.

Great, timeless stories weave this powerful human truth throughout their plots. *Superman. It's A Wonderful Life. Hunger Games.* The power of redemption is a wonderful theme to start with when deciding what to write about. My novel *Dreadlands* incorporates the theme of redemption, even so much as to focus on the shedding of innocent blood in order for life to continue; for survival. My basic story is the Biblical redemption story. But the plot is about a boy who leads his sister across a Norse realm to the city by the sea before shifting wolves leave the Dreadlands on the next full moon. Yup, Viking and werewolves overlaying the skeleton of redemption. This story comes to life in its own world.

"In the Beginning" focuses a lot on world building. The first thing God does is create a clear time and place for our story to take place in. The story world rules are established. The order of life is stated. And the characters aren't introduced until the world is complete.

As a writer, it is crucial that your reader quickly understand the story world. When and where does the story take place? If it's speculative fiction, what are the rules or lure of this world? If it's historical, what changes alter or prohibit the characters from making the same choices you would make? Many authors begin with dialogue or story problem too quickly, and the reader gets lost, not having been grounded in the story world first. Check out the first paragraph of *The Hunger Games* by Suzanne Collins from Scholastic Books. What does the beginning tell us?

- They are not rich. For this character to be sharing a bed with a sibling, they are probably scraping by in this society.
- Rough canvas cover of the mattress means this is not present day America. It is either very long

ago or set in a post-apocalyptic or dystopian future (or a different world altogether).

- Wherever this is, it's a scary, unstable world for this little girl to have recurring nightmares.

Dad's either dead or gone because she climbed in with 'our mother', not 'our parents.'

The Day of the Reaping sounds horrible when connected to nightmares. Reaping means "to harvest the crop" (Merriam Webster Dictionary). The only crop that could induce nightmares would be human or animal, because not too many people get scared of picking apples. This also lets me know we're not in the past because the Day of the Reaping doesn't exist.

The world is already clearly established in the first paragraph. Not completely, but enough for me to follow. I know where we are, when, the mood, and time, and that's so important for your readers.

The Bible shows in Genesis 1 verse 2, "The Earth was without form and void, and darkness was upon the face of the deep. And the Spirit of God moved upon the face of the waters."

So our world stared with nothing, an empty, unformed place that God populated in a particular order. To see the new world, he created light; Day and Night. He established time, a crucial component for your story world. When does your story take place? Past, present future? Day, night? Winter, summer?

Then God created the world, separating the Heaven from the Earth. He created boundaries. Does your universe have clearly marked boundaries for your reader? Is it the size of a bedroom or beyond the known universe?

Next, came land and sea, two distinct settings in the story. Where does your story take place? Are the locations clearly marked for your reader? God showed the details of the setting; the grass and herbs and how they continued their existence by containing seeds to reproduce. Trees producing fruit is an awesome foreshadow to the Garden of Eden story.

Now, God created the sun and moon, the stars, the universe beyond the world. Your story needs to appear larger than the people where the narrative takes place. Your reader may never see beyond the world you create, but they must believe the map keeps growing beyond your story's borders.

The setting is now complete. A world exists. A universe grows beyond the world. The world is self-sustained. Now what? According to the Author of the World, it is time to populate it and set up a hierarchy of order.

In Genesis 1:20, sea creatures were born. In verse 21, birds flew in the sky. Since most of the Bible stories take place on land, I think it's interesting that water and sky creatures are introduced first. I liken them to background fillers, those characters that exist in your story world to make it more believable, but don't move the story forward. In *The Hunger Games*, that would be the Peacemakers, the merchants in the Hob, and the miners. They are all apart of District 12, but they aren't where the story takes place. Does your story have filler characters or entities that live in your story world but don't necessarily drive the plot?

Next, God created every creature on the land. These animals provide food, shelter, clothing, and companionship for mankind. They keep the bug population down so man can grow crops. They fertilize the soil. They plow the fields. They are integral to man's existence. Do you have elements in your story world that keep your society functioning? Is their a believable hierarchy in your story world?

Finally, God had the stage set. He was ready to create the main character: Man. Man had the main dominion of this new world, charged to take care of it and protect its inhabitants. And like your main character, man was created in the author's image. After all, you are the god of your story world. You have provided the perfect environment for your characters to thrive in. But beware. There is a serpent with other plans slithering through your perfect world, waiting for just the right moment to strike.

Chapter Two:

The Villain and the Vixen

When does the villain show up in the story? When everything seems just right. When the world is established. When the love interest comes along.

After creation, God rested. Why? Was He tired? Did He have a busy day He needed to rest up for? Of course, not. He's God! In the sense of story, it seems like the perfect place for the reader to pause and catch their breath; to revel in the beauty and perfection of the story world, like Dorothy landing in Oz. But the wicked witch lurked in the shadows waiting to strike, as does the serpent in Eden, waiting for just the right character to enter the scene and release chaos into the perfect world.

Let's back up in the text and see what other writing tools are used. In verse five, God mentions how He hasn't caused it to rain yet. Why? As a reader, we know rain is a part of life. It cleanses the Earth and sustains all life. God provides a mist to cleanse and sustain. He was the source. This is an important new rule for our story world. Why? Because it foreshadows to the story of Noah. It is a simple line in chapter two, yet it provides a double-edged sword of meaning for the reader:

1. The rain will come
2. God is the sole provider for this world

Next, God talks specifically about the creation of Adam and Eve. From dust, God breathed life and created the first Biblical character. In verse seven, God "breathed into his nostrils the breath of life." What an awesome illustration of our role as author. Our job is to breathe life into our characters, not to just mold them from clay. They need to be complex, realistic entities with a spirit and a soul, not just a body.

What makes us human? What separates us from animals?

*   Humor
*   Appreciation of beauty
*   Self-consciousness
*   Awareness of death
*   Understanding time
*   Meaning of life
*   Malleability
*   Lack of harmony with nature
*   A sense of morality
*   Character
*   Free moral agency

- Capacity for wisdom
- Desire to worship
- Love

(www.realtruth.org)

If your characters don't exhibit varying degrees of many or all of these traits, they are simply animals wearing human skin and clothing. This skill takes time to cultivate, but by reading books and observing what makes a character great, you will soon develop it. I like to study actors when I watch films to see the dynamics of their flaws. To me, it helps me to translate these inconsistencies into my own characters.

After verse 7, the chapter goes into a detailed description of the Garden of Eden, its rivers and boundaries; its resources and trees; ah, yes…the trees of Eden. One contained the entire knowledge of all things good and evil. The other contained the answer to eternal life. How many stories have been built on those premises? The *Indiana Jones* franchise. *Journey to the Center of the Earth. The Time Machine.* The trees are neutral, like the red and blue pills in *The Matrix*, but the consequences of the choices are purely owned by the beholder. In your stories, you need to have those "trees" which tempt and lead the character into forced decisions. They must dangle as lures desensitizing your characters by becoming a familiar place within the story world and therefore less ominous. ("My precious…")

Your main character may have the will power to face his task and not be easily swayed. He, like Adam, does what he was created to do, day in and day out. So here's where you throw in the wrench. Adam, amidst all this perfection and beauty, became lonely. He had no one to share it with; no one to enjoy the journey and grow with.

Enter the love interest.

Lois Lane. Rhett Butler. Augustus Waters.

The love interest brings out the main characters weaknesses. They can either be oblivious to their impact or diabolical in their strategy. Their role, as illustrated by Eve, is to play helper and fill in something that is missing within the main character. "And they shall be one flesh," verse 24. This doesn't mean your book must mirror the *50 Shades*; it's more of a "You complete me" *Jerry Maguire* kind of one-flesh.

Take some time to dissect and list the pluses and the minuses, the positive traits and the negative ones between the main character and the love interest in your favorite stories. Don't be surprised to discover that where one is a two for shyness, the other is an 8 for outgoing. Where one is a three for compassion, the other is a seven for tolerance. Build these traits into your characters and flip them in the love interest. You'll provide both deep-felt connections and hostile contradictions within their relationship, which makes for believability and, more importantly, relatability for your reader.

In Genesis chapter three, the villain enters; stage right. "Now the serpent was more subtle than any beast of the field which the Lord God had made." (verse 1) Interestingly, God points out that he deliberately created this creature. Your villain also is a reflection of you, of your upbringing, prejudices, biases, and experiences, if only the flipside. When my villains appear, I may ask myself, "What *wouldn't* I do in this situation?" or "What could this character do that would be the most horrible thing imaginable?" These answers are based in my beliefs and convictions. Why? Because I created my villain.

In Eden, the serpent heads straight to Eve, twists God's words just enough to enter doubt, then sits back to watch. Eve forfeits her fate. Why does this method work? Because a partial truth is always easier to believe than a flat out lie. Your characters are smart. Your readers are smarter. The partial truth—"This is just a game, Ender"—is easier to swallow. We want to believe it's the whole truth so badly that we override our common sense to satisfy our immediate wants. That's human nature, and that's what the serpent toyed with. The betrayal worked because Eve chose to believe she was being shafted by God. If the serpent had told her, "You'll gain ultimate knowledge and realize there are evils in the world beyond your comprehension, find yourself banished, and experience horrible pain during childbirth," she wouldn't have taken the fruit. Again, the questions from *The Matrix* rings true: the red or the blue pill?

This form of deception is seen in Frodo's quest in *Lord of the Rings* and Harry Potter's journey to defeat Lord Voldemort. Both Frodo and Harry are fed just enough of the truth to hook them and bring them to the dark truth of what they were really getting involved with. Both stories are brilliant and powerfully written, utilizing the very writing tool showcased in the Garden of Eden between the villain and the vixen.

Chapter Three:

Conflict

The story of Cain and Abel could be presented as a tragic dysfunctional family gone awry. You've got murder, jealousy, betrayal, pride, greed, agony, banishment, and isolation all rolled up into a single story. How anyone could find the Old Testament boring or irrelevant is beyond me. This sounds like the makings of a Hollywood blockbuster, a national bestseller, or a reality TV show waiting to be penned.

Let's set the scene: Adam and Eve have been banished from Eden, forced to till the ground for the first time ever in order to survive. Can you imagine the dinner conversations in this home? "Sorry dinner is late, Eve. Would have come sooner if you hadn't given me that fruit to eat." "Me? You're the one that was so lonely he needed someone. I came from your rib, you know, so it's your fault."

We don't see any of this banter, of course,

because it is back-story and not all back-story needs to be written. Much of it can be inferred from the narrative or dialogue, which keeps the story driving forward. In this chapter, a new story world exists, one in which weeds must be picked, animals must be sacrificed, and child birth is painful.

Let's pause on the sacrifice for a moment. When Adam was given charge of the animals, he became their father. The Bible says he knew them by name. (Genesis 2:19) When sin entered the garden and Adam and Eve realized they were naked, they covered themselves with leaves. But what did God do? He killed an animal, skinned it, and used its hide to make clothes. How horrible! Imagine skinning your dog or cat and using their fur for clothing. That would be a close equivalent to what Adam and Eve were going through.

God removes the leaves and replaces them with flesh. He sets up new rules for the new story world: innocent blood sacrifice covers sin.

Adam and Eve tried to cover their sin (shame) with plants.

God commanded that their sin (shame) could only be covered with sacrifice.

So going into this new world outside of the garden, there is only one sacrifice God will accept: blood atonement.

As your story world is altered by conflict, change is inevitable. The rules of Kansas don't apply in Oz. Muggles adhere to different boundaries and limitations than do witches and wizards inside Hogwarts. And the rules in Narnia are completely different than those in World War II England. Have you created unique story worlds where rules change with conflict? It is a subtle yet key element between a story that works and a story you can't put down.

In Genesis chapter four, Cain the farmer and his brother Abel the shepherd, both bring of their talents and offer sacrifices to the Lord. Cain's harvest offering is denied while Abel's blood sacrifice is accepted. Cain becomes furious. His jealousy grows into envy, and then from rage to hatred. As an observer, we wonder why. The established rule was that plants were not good enough and God only accepted animal sacrifice. ("Four feet good, two feet bad") Why was Cain so angry? All he had to do was follow the rules.

But rules are made to be broken.

In your story world, the clearer the rules, the easier they will be to break. Having either an antagonist or protagonist break them will naturally result in conflict spilling over from human emotions. Take a look at the story rules and how they are handled by the protagonist and antagonist of several of your favorite stories. By breaking the rules, what human emotion naturally swells and what level of conflict does this create? Now, take a look at your own story. Are your story rules clearly established? How can the protagonist or antagonist break them and to what affect? What emotions result from these choices? And how can you use those emotions to escalate tension in the story?

In the story of Cain and Abel, the act of sacrificing fruits and vegetables (breaking the rules) resulted in God's displeasure and rejection (consequence). Cain becomes jealous, envious, determined, angry, then full of hate (emotional result) causing him to murder his own brother (tension escalation).

Now what?

God comes down and asks Cain where Abel is, and Cain answers, "Am I my brother's keeper?" (verse 9) God curses Cain, banishing him from ever finding a permanent home and preventing the ground from providing for him anymore. Again, the story world has been altered by the addition of conflict.

In *Jumanji* by Chris van Allsburg, the town changes every time the dice is thrown. With each additional conflict, the character's emotional stakes raise, resulting in a need to handle the new story problem differently than the last one. This can be seen in his other book *Zathura*, where the consequences of each spin add to the tension and emotion while the rules of the story world are altered.

If your story world looks the same on page one as it does on the last page, you may need to clarify the rules of your story world. Then, find ways that either the antagonist or protagonist can break them, upping the tension and resulting in an altered story world for the characters to figure out.

In my book *Exposure*, I incorporated the mark of Cain and his curse of wandering the Earth into my story rules. The story didn't start out with Cain as the premise, but by adding these rules from the Bible into my own story rules, it added tension, plot twist, and emotion to my novel. Here's what the story is about:

When a boy loses his parents and finds a roll a film in a strange town, he'll discover the photographs reveal clues that lead him to believe his parents are still alive somewhere, but the town won't let him leave until he figures it all out.

Tember Asch is sent to live in a small beach town without so much as a McDonalds to keep him company. But nothing is as it should be. He sees things that aren't there, and discovers a roll of film in his drawer that he knows wasn't there before. He heads to a town to have the film developed but once he's there, the town won't let him go. Like Alice in Wonderland, he is trapped in a world that makes no sense as he seeks a way home. Along the way he finds other kids brought to the town only they all share a similar mark. The Mark of Cain. They have been brought here to die, only no one knows who brought Tember to the town or why.
Exposure, a deadly game filled with twisted characters and clues that must be solved before anyone can go home.

The plot of brother against brother is timeless. I mean, who doesn't love a little sibling rivalry? The need to be accepted by family, especially by our parents, is in all of us. Some people spend their whole lives seeking this approval and never find it, even after their parents are dead. Through the wrong lens, this favoritism can easily cause one sibling to detest the other.

The Dursley's behave this way in *Harry Potter*, favoring Dudley in grotesquely overdone behavior. Luke Skywalker learns Darth Vader is his father and faces a serious choice that raises tension in the story. The characters in *Holes* all face mommy and daddy issues. *The Lemonade War. Cinder. Beezus and*

Ramona. All of these stories take the timeless tool of sibling rivalry with just the right twist to create story problems. Utilizing the need to be accepted by parents sprinkled with sibling favoritism can create intense story problems and consequences between your characters, just like it did with the Cain and Abel.

And now that the rules have been broken, your story will flow like clockwork!

Chapter Four:

The Hero

The Bible is filled with stories of heroes, the greatest of whom being Jesus Christ. The hero's plight connects us to one another; we can see both our own strengths and weaknesses simultaneously played out within the hero's choices and shortcomings. Who doesn't want to know that somewhere, someone has it all under control, and if we need help, help is on its way? It's a bird, it's a plane, no, it's Superman! See any resemblance between the Man of Steel and the Son of Man? Both were sent from another place by their father to save humanity. Both loved mankind, even unto death. Both possessed super-human strength and powers greater than mortal man. Superman was modeled after Jesus' life even down to his name: Kal-el meaning "voice of God" in Hebrew.

The first hero of the Bible is Noah, the guy who built the ark. But that's not how it starts. Let's bring in the back-story and set the scene first, so our hero's journey will make sense. It was still a world where water sprung from the ground. Rain had not been "invented" yet. It was also a time when women fornicated with the sons of God, or the Nephilim – a crossbreed of men and fallen angels. They were monstrous and god-like. Giants. And through them, mankind grew evil.

The scene is set, be it Mordor or Gotham City, and it's ripe for a hero.

God's heart was grieved [Genesis 6:6] and he decided to destroy the Earth and everything that populated it. Hit delete. Crumple up the page. Back to the drawing board. "But Noah found grace in the eyes of the Lord." (Verse 8)

Haven't you written this story before? You are going along in the story world you've created with great characters and story twists, when suddenly you realize that the story has gone in its own direction as if its own entity without your assistance. What do you do? How can you fix it? Many times, you feel you can't, and the delete button calls to you. Or if you write freehand, like I do, the paper shredder taunts of its insatiable hunger. You could drawer the book, but even then, you know the story is no longer your own, having been hijacked by your characters. And just when all seems lost, one character won't stop talking to you, won't get out of your head.

"I can fix this," it whispers.

And you know at that moment, a hero has been born.

The corrupt world is an awesome opportunity to have a hero rise from the ashes. It's what pushes Katniss Everdeen and Harry Potter and Bruce Wayne and Clark Kent. Justice. The people are weak or sheltered or afraid of those who hold power over them. A dysfunctional homeostasis has been reached. Someone needs to tip the scales for the greater good.

What elements of oppression and despair have you built into your story world and characters? Can you kick it up a notch or layer it on a grander scale so it isn't just about a boy who loses his parents but also about a city that has lost all hope?

In verse 14 of Genesis 4, God gives Noah "The Plan." He forewarns of Earth's imminent destruction and tells him to build an ark to save himself, his family, and the creatures God would send. Remember that foreshadow to rain? Here it is again, but coming to pass in story time. A flood is coming. A major calamity that will destroy almost everything but that which is carried in the ark.

Imagine the ridicule and isolation, the moments of self-doubt; the fear, from not only Noah but his family, who trusted him blindly with their lives. In *Ender's Game*, Ender Wiggins commands a fleet to destroy an 'evil' alien planet by wiping it off the map. His crew follows his revolutionary orders, while Ender's commanders watch in horror. They all trust him, both those who think it's a game and those who know better.

The hero leads to victory. He doesn't question his orders. He doesn't try to please anyone but his own innate gut. And he never stops short of ultimate victory. Game over. The stakes are on the hero's shoulders. All failures are ultimately his.

With the element of rain thrown into the mix, Noah had an even stronger faith than most. It had never rained before. Chicken Little, the sky is falling! What elements can you throw into your story to greaten the hero's plight? Changing the rules is precarious, because there still needs to be a strong level of believability or else you risk losing your reader. But done correctly, the tension and stakes raise dramatically, drawing your character from the crowd to the hero's circle.

The other story element God introduces with this chapter is the ticking time bomb. Time is set and will eventually run out. The first thriller. If you can utilize time as a threat, it always boosts the hero's journey. She must make hard, split-second decisions. She must stay focused at all costs. She must reach the climax before time runs out. So many stories incorporate this device. Perhaps the most well-known is Cinderella. "You have till midnight." Creating an environment and plot that go against the grain with a life or death outcome by a certain time will guarantee the rise of a hero. And like God showed through Genesis Chapter six, it just might save the world from final deletion.

Chapter Five:

Let it Rain!

As a good parent, you want what's best for your children. You want to help when you can, wipe their tears, and make their road through life as easy as possible. As the creator of your characters, this type of treatment makes for extremely boring literature. The more problems and chaos and rain you can throw at your characters, the better! As Stephen King puts it, throw characters into a difficult situation and watch them squirm out of it.

In Genesis, chapter seven, time has run out for Noah. The animals have arrived, two-by-two, and God has shut them in the ark. (verse 16) "And God opened the windows of heaven and broke the fountains of the great deep" (verse 11) flooding the Earth for forty days and forty nights before the storm subsided. God kept his word providing safekeeping for Noah, his family, and the animals, and death for every living thing outside of the ark.

As a reader, we feel satisfied. A flood was predicted. A flood came.

Was it easy for Noah? No way. Regardless of the ridicule and torment prior to the flood, that first drop of rain fell as his confirmation letter from heaven. The people knew. His family knew. Noah knew. Imagine the cries of those outside the ark, pounding their fists against the gopher wood, staring through the air slats, grappling with the winds and waves, begging for forgiveness and entrance.

It would have been easy for God to say, "Okay. You learned your lesson. Everybody, out of the boat. I'm turning off the faucet."

But then what?

We would have been left with an unfinished story. No lesson would have been learned. No true repentance can come when a decision is based in fear.

As your story 'god' you cannot make it easy for your characters when they are facing the consequences of their choices. You can't reach down and scoop them up as the floods come. No, quite the contrary. You must raise the flood water so high that the mountaintops are covered, leaving your characters riding the swells, praying they'll make it out alive. You cannot lower the stakes. That's where the story is! That's where your character's true colors show, just like in real life. You must make it rain.

In the *Wizard of Oz*, Glenda visits Dorothy in Munchkinland. What if she had flown her to the Emerald City and the Wizard had sent her home immediately? Better still, what if she had clicked her heels together three times the moment she stepped into the ruby slippers? Dorothy would have just gone back home to her same disappointments and troubles. She wouldn't have learned any lessons. But having her face the Wicked Witch of the West, help her new friends grow, watch her only ride float away without her, all the while thinking Auntie Em had died or given up hope, Dorothy's heart changes. She regrets running away and wanting to leave home. She realizes that if it isn't in her own backyard then she didn't need it to begin with. The repentant heart. A changed spirit. After all, there's no place like home.

Have you rescued your hero instead of letting him face the consequences of his choices? Have you made it too easy for her to succeed? Where can you make it rain? What crutch could you take away that would raise the floodwaters? Let the hero have the opportunity to rescue the day, but not until after she slays a dragon or two.

Chapter Six:

The Power of Threes

Have you ever noticed that jokes are delivered in threes? First guy does something, second guy does something even bigger, but the third guy delivers the punch line. Or that one knock-knock joke about a banana and an orange, where you really are glad by the third knock that he didn't say banana. Threes hold power in writing and in life. Beginning, middle, end; sky, land, sea; child, adult, senior.

As I was reading Genesis chapter 8, I noticed Noah sent the dove out three different times in search of dry land. The first time, she returned empty-handed (verse 9). The second time, she brought Noah an olive leaf (verse11). And finally, in verse 12, he sends out the dove and she never returns.

Why include all of that in the text? Why not sum it up that after some time, Noah sent out a dove and she didn't return? What's the point? By setting it up this way, I think it adds to the believability and the tension in the story build up. Each time that dove flies away, you hope alongside Noah that it will not return. When it comes back empty-handed, you share in Noah's fear, hopelessness, disappointment, even claustrophobia. What if the waters never recede? The second time, when the dove returns with the leaf in her beak, you find excitement swells inside of you. "It won't be long now!" And finally, when she leaves for good, there's relief and celebration after all the tension dissolves. From riding the storm to watching humanity wiped away, when the dove doesn't come back you realize that it's finally over.

Three holds a cadence in our psyche. *Three Little Pigs. Goldilocks and the Three Bears. The Three Billy Goats Gruff.*

"Two's company; three's a crowd."

"Three strikes, you're out!"

"Three-two-one-blast off!"

God even formed us in his image with a spirit, soul (mind/heart), and body matching the Godhead of God the Father, God the Son, and God the Holy Spirit.

So Noah with his wife and three sons with their three wives (there's that power of threes again) leave the ark in verse 16. And God commands everyone to be fruitful and multiply, including all the fowl, cattle, and creeping things.

There are threes everywhere in this chapter.

The problem comes when you force the threes, making your writing sound mechanical and formulaic, inorganic in much the same way as someone who is bad at telling jokes missing the punch line.

Where have you used the power of threes naturally in your story? Can you bring it out more to connect with your reader? Do you have a clear opening and closing to the three acts of your narrative? There should be a definitive set up period, confrontation section, and a final resolution.

Let's really take a look at the power of threes in structure. In the first act, the exposition establishes the main characters and their relationships to the world around them. We are introduced to our protagonist who is forced into Act II through an inciting incident and the point of no return. Three elements: establish, incite, and turning point.

Act II is where the bulk of the story takes place, but without an inciting incident, you and your reader will never arrive here. This should be the longest part of the story and include organic elements of the power of threes. Try-fail, try-fail, try-succeed.

Act III concludes the story with climax, falling action, and resolution. Again, three distinct movements that define this section of a story. Pretty amazing, huh?

Noah's story continues with the animal sacrifice to thank God for his favor and safety to which God replies with a rainbow to seal his promise that he would never destroy all life again through a flood.

I think it's fascinating how God makes these promises to mankind, not because we are deserving of them, but "...for man's sake; for the imagination of mans' heart is evil from youth." (Genesis 8:21) Right then, God knew we would soon forget his wrath and punishment, and be right back to our old evil ways before we knew it.

It's interesting here, with the power of threes, how God decides to wipe out humanity, but saves Noah for a remnant to begin again. Then, he says it later with Moses, how he would kill all the Israelites in the Wilderness whom he'd just delivered out of Egypt because of their blatant disobedience, offering to keep Moses alive and start again. Of course, it doesn't happen because Moses pleads on behalf of the people, but we still see God's desire to wipe out sin by destroying mankind on two occasions. Now to the punch line. Finally, the third time is the crucifixion. Here, we witness Jesus bearing the entire sins of humanity into death, separated from his father, on our behalf and battling for Death's keys three days and three nights. Our resurrected savior is the result of God's third and final attempt to wipe out sin and death. Try-fail, try-fail, try-succeed. Through the blood of the Lamb, we can all live again. Now *that's* the power of threes!

Chapter Seven:

Foreshadowing Through Character

Skipping ahead a few chapters, we reach Genesis chapter 12. Are those chapters in between irrelevant? No, of course, not. They talk of the rainbow after the flood, the lineage of Noah and his sons, the building of the Tower of Babel, the introduction of the nations, and the existence of Abram and his wife, Sarai.

Reading those pages of who begot who can be tiresome, but its still important. In fact, I once diagrammed the family tree from Adam to Noah by birth, age, and death year to see who knew who. Here's what I learned: Methuselah was alive when Adam was alive. As a little boy, he probably sat on great-great-great-grandpa Adam's lap hearing firsthand accounts of God in the Garden of Eden and the importance of obedience. These stories were not hearsay, but directly from the horses' mouth. 900+

29

years later, great-great-great-grandpa Methuselah passes these stories down through the generations to Noah himself; secondhand information, probably mostly accurate, with some embellishments.

Methuselah, who walked with Adam, was the oldest and last to die of Adam's direct lineage. He died the year of the flood. So everyone from Adam to Noah's dad were dead before the floodwaters rose. And Noah carried on the legacy of Creation with the stories from Adam to Methuselah.

Remember this the next time you feel like breezing over all those names. They do have a purpose, or they wouldn't be in the Bible. Sometimes, you just have to dig deeper to find the connection.

So with that, we're gonna skip over the chapters with all those names (tee-hee) and get into some foreshadowing through the first of many stories of Abram. In verse 2 of Genesis 12, God tells Abram, "I will make of thee a great nation." Here he is, old as dirt and childless, yet God says he'll be the father of a great nation, which means millions of people.

In verse three, we read, "and in thee shall all families of the earth be blessed."

Could this be our foreshadow to the stubbornness of the Israelites and the fulfillment of Messiah? Probably. Even before the nation exists, God knows his chosen people will rebel to the point of denial.

Abram is instructed to leave the land of his father, journey through the land God promises to give him, and into Egypt to escape a great famine, for Egypt was the mightiest nation of the day.

Right before they enter Egypt, Abram tells Sarai

to lie and say she's his sister. Why? Because she is so beautiful, Abram is afraid he will be killed so the Pharaoh can take Sarai, who by the way is over sixty, as his wife. (She was technically his sister by blood, so it was more of the omission of truth than a flat out lie, but you get the gist.) She must have been one hot mama to put such fear in her husband's heart. And Abram wasn't being biased because she *was* taken into the Pharaoh's house due to her great beauty. (verse 15) Abram is given cattle and oxen and sheep and camels and servants and maids, all on behalf of his "sister." Until Pharaoh learns the truth. Then they are both sent away for fear of God's wrath upon Egypt.

Okay, let's check out the foreshadowing here. First, there's a famine that is so great people flood Egypt for food. Sounds a lot like the story of Jacob, Abram's grandson, to come in later chapters. Second, Pharaoh sends them away for fear of God's wrath, which occurs. "And the Lord plagued Pharaoh and his house with great plagues because of Sarai, Abram's wife." (verse 17) Ever heard of a guy named Moses? Ten plagues? Red Sea parting? Am I ringing any bells?

Finally, this exact event occurs in Abram's son's life, Isaac.

Let me explain: Isaac marries Rebekah, who is technically his cousin, and goes to Egypt to escape a famine, where he instructs his wife to say she's his sister, because she is so beautiful, he fears Pharaoh will kill him for his wife, yada...yada...yada.

I love that third one.

Foreshadowing is such a powerful tool when paralleling story and character. Small changes can draw a huge connection later in the story through plot, character, or both, that layer your story to grow beyond a surface relationship with the reader to something so powerful that it creates a classic.

Holes by Louis Sachar works this brilliantly through the parallel of past and present with Kissing Kate and the "no-good-dirty-rotten-pig-stealing-great-great-grandfather." *Star Wars* foreshadows Luke's flirting with the Dark Side and following in his father's footsteps, only to break out not only himself but Anakin in the end. "The sins of the father" is a powerful foreshadowing tool. Generational curses or repeating the mistakes of the family create great tension as your character battles between his fate and trying to change it. Redemption tastes that much sweeter when your character manages to break the family curse and create a new path for the next generation.

The *Back to the Future* trilogy is riddled with the use of foreshadow and the sins of the father. The diner and clock tower and head bumps are staples that draw the parallel universes into common ground.

What similarities can you draw between your character's journey and plot points throughout your story? How can you accentuate those choices to impact the plot even greater?

In Stephen King's book *On Writing* he mentions the thread of blood that appeared in his novel *Carrie*. He hadn't intended to, but there was blood present at every major plot point in the book. By editing the accidental coincidences and turning them into purposed foreshadowing, *Carrie* launched his career and became a story that resonates with readers' years after they finish reading it.

Utilize what's already in your story to make connections and foreshadows that will impact your reader. Find those loose threads and tie them together to create layers that deepen your theme, plot, and relationship with your audience.

Chapter Eight:

Tension and Strife

Genesis 13 begins with a now wealthy Abram and his nephew, Lot—who was equally wealthy—leaving Egypt and heading back to the land God promised Abram. (verses 1-5) They set up camp, pitch their tents, and fall into their daily routine. It's human nature to claim your spot and fill it with your things.

But what happens when your uncle loses his house and he and his family move in? What do they do? Uncle helps Dad finally straighten out the garage, where he sets up a cot and creates a 'man cave' while Auntie helps Mom in the garden by day and has a happy home in the spare bedroom-office by night. And that no-good kid of theirs doesn't do anything, except make a mess that you get blamed for, play video games, and oh yeah, share a room with you. Suddenly, your trophies have been displaced, your clothes wedged into one drawer, and there's a hand towel and a rolled up pair of socks on the floor for your new bed.

And the fighting begins.

You are on edge, waiting for a turn in the bathroom, trying to steal back your bed, and hurrying to get the last piece of bacon so at least you can say you had one. What happened? Your home used to be so peaceful, and according to the conversations you've overheard between Dad and Uncle, your cousin has never been confrontational before (tell that to the big welt on the back of your thigh).

The problem is there's not enough room for two families to live under the same roof. This is a guarantee for strife. There are two ways of doing things, two sets of rules, two expectations, not to mention space constraints, daily routine, and clashing personalities.

In Bill Allen's book *Orson Buggy's The Big Fang Theory* the bully's mom marries Orson's dad, and they not only move in together, but they boys have to share a bedroom. What a mess! Privacy is gone and Orson fears for his life.

In Genesis 13:7, Lot's herdsmen and Abram's herdsmen are filled with strife. "That's our watering hole" or "Our cattle were eating here first." Day in and day out, this escalates into physical altercations. Complaining, fighting, and discourse fill the whole area. And you know how people tend to get more riled up when they are part of a group then when they are on their own. Look at *Lord of the Flies*.

The cool thing about this section is that the two families were living on the ground God had promised Abram. But how did he resolve the issue? He let Lot choose where he wanted to make camp and Abram would take what was left. Wow. No way would I do that. Of course, Lot chose the greenest grass near the water, the most ideal location for his herdsmen and their families to start their community. Only the plain of Jordan faced Sodom, and this is where Lot pitched his tent. (verse 12)

There's two great writing truths to be taken from this chapter. First, get your people in the same place, to need the same things, and strife will naturally follow. *Goldilocks and the Three Bears. Divergent. Rita Hayworth and the Shawshank Redemption.* If they are forced to share a car or a tent or one of them loses everything and is forced to rely on the other (*The Life of Pi*), you will provide organic opportunity for your characters to react to the world around them. Want to see who's really inside someone? Make them uncomfortable, and then take away their security and control. You'll see the true hearts of your characters, and it may not be so pretty.

The other truth is the idea of placing beauty within walking distance of bad things; bringing the two into the same room. The plain of Jordan was part of God's promised land. It was the most beautiful part, with lush green grass and cool springs. But it was positioned at Sodom's door. "But the men of Sodom were wicked and sinners before the Lord exceedingly." (verse 13) Amidst the beauty, lay wickedness.

When you can show those extremes attempting to coexist in your work, you will evoke strong emotions from your readers. Don't believe me? Try these images: The beauty of Oz in full Technicolor and then BAM! Black smoke and it's shattered by the presence of the Wicked Witch of the West. Or Hobbits and dwarves and elves (oh my!) in Rivendell, then

BAM! Vile Orcs, broken bodies, and bloodied rivers. Or what about Pinocchio heading over to Pleasure Island? Sounds like a juvenile version of Lot and Sodom, but instead of having a nose that grows with lies, there's a wife who turns into a pillar of salt with her eyes.

Beauty + Evil = Fear.

Plain and simple.

Find places in your book to add fear and strife through contradictory settings and heart squeezing scenes. Put unlikely characters close, then force them closer. Take everything away that makes them comfortable and then stand back and watch. Tension and strife are bound to happen. Just be close by ready to write them out of it at the very last moment.

Chapter Nine:

Back-story and Clichés

If you want to learn how to write battle scenes, the Old Testament should be your guide. Genesis chapter 14 is like reading a scene out of Tolkien's classic parallel story "The Ring of the Lord." There's great lure, providing just the right amount of back-story in verses 1-4. I mean, check out this great opener: "And it came to pass in the days of Amraphel king of Shinar, Arioch king of Ellasar, Chedorlaomer king of Elam, and Tidal king of nations;" (verse 1) See what I mean? What great names for an epic fantasy novel.

So these five kings make war with "Bera king of Sodom, and with Birsha king of Gomorrah, Shinab king of Admah, and Shemeber king of Zeborim, and the king of Bela, which is Zoar." (verse 2)

Imagine the vast armies, each robed in their own colors, waving the crest of their king, astride horses and camels with foot soldiers and artillery facing off "in the vale of Siddim" (the Salt Sea). That would make an awesome novel, and the title is built right in: In the Vale of Siddim.

Verse 4 continues with the back-story of how the people served Chedorlaomer for twelve years, rebelled in the thirteenth year, and were smote by Chedorlaomer and his allies in the fourteenth year. In the movie version, this would be the intro-dubbed over by the narrator, letting the audience know the events leading up to the moment our story begins, like they do in *300* and *Lord of the Rings*.

As a writer, it can be tricky to start a book with relevant back story or prologue in most cases. It's easy for the writing to come across "telling" or "teaching" and the audience feels a great distance from the narrative. Plus, the reader has no vested interest yet. There is no main character to cheer for or any emotional ties established because the story hasn't started yet. So how do you deliver back-story without losing the reader? Let's see how the great author accomplished it.

This story in chapter 14 involves Abram, Lot, and the promises God makes to Abram. These are elements we already know because Abram enters the scene way back in chapter 11, along with Lot, and the pinkie swear occurs first thing in chapter 12. We get characters, relationships, story problems, and setting well-grounded way before we take this segway into epic battles and many kings.

In my novel *Dreadlands* there is a book containing a prophecy that strings the story together, but I didn't share the ancient text on page one or in an unnecessary prologue. I didn't even let the main character, Arud, open the book when he first discovered it. I waited until the story was moving along and needed a break to introduce the back-story over several different chapters, not in one sitting.

Author Davis Bunn teaches that your story should open as a door that the reader must run through to catch up. That is rarely if ever accomplished with a prologue or back-story. Movies, of course, are different. *Star Wars* uses the opening scene of each film to display written narrative back-story, and it works. The same is true of *Hunger Games* and *The Teenage Mutant Ninja Turtles* film. The exception? Sequels. Book two can break the back-story rule. Why? Vested interest. The reader is back, which means they care.

Take a look at your work-in-progress. Have you opened the scene in a moment or a memory? What information can you cut out and paste back into the story in small snippets after the story problem and characters are established? How much of the back-story is for you, the author, to understand the characters and problems? Is it necessary for the reader to know this information?

If you notice in chapter 14, we aren't given the reason why this epic battle started. Did the author know why? You better believe it. But he determined the reader didn't need to know. It's crucial to know what is for you and what is for your reader. That's why I believe most prologues are unnecessary for the reader, and when I'm editing a book for a client I take prologues out almost every time. In fact, 9 times out of 10 you can read, understand, and enjoy the novel without ever needing to know a single detail from a prologue.

In verse 12 we discover Lot has been taken. Now our story starts. Why? Because our main characters, Lot and Abram, are involved. Abram is given a message by someone who escaped the great battle in the Valley of Siddim that Lot and his belongings have been stolen from Sodom, where Lot lives. So Uncle Abram goes in like Rambo with a guerilla crew of 318 of his personal guard and "smote them." (defined: defeat or conquer; attack severely-Webster's Dictionary) Not only does Abram return his nephew and his nephew's belongings, but he brings back "all the goods,...and the women also, and the people" back to the king of Sodom.

I love this side of Abram; face painted in desert camo, girded with daggers and shields, sneaking into camp in the middle of the night, and slitting his enemy's throats. That's my kind of story! I know some of you just cringed, but you have to understand when you read these Old Testament tales that this is what they're about. Images of peaceful patriarchs with flowing white beards don't match up to the truth of the ruthlessness of the day and age in which they lived.

What can we learn from that as writers? The folly of the cliché.

It's so easy to fall into the trap: the dumb jock, the blonde bimbo, the shy nerd, and the sweet girl-next-door. Shake things up! Characters that break the mold are far more likely to stick with your reader. Think about Shrek and Monk and Ender Wiggins. These characters are the wrong species, have psychological issues, or are way too young to be playing their roles. But they work brilliantly.

Where have you written lazy cliché characters?

How can you adjust or change them to break the mold and create unique, organic characters your reader won't forget? Remember, your story is original and so you should populate it with original characters that are provided with just enough back-story to engage the reader while pushing the plot forward.

Chapter Ten:

The Sidekick

In this chapter we will review Genesis chapter 15 to see how character roles can affect the protagonist. There are two main influences in Abram's life: the Lord God and Sarai his wife. I believe it's safe to assume that both love Abram, want the best for Abram, and support Abram. This is how it should be with those in your inner circle. I'm sure you have a few close friends whose opinions and advice you esteem, who you lean on and trust. Your characters should also. And just like in real life, where people who you love can still hurt you, your character's friends, confidants, and mentors shouldn't be static and can shift into the roles of antagonists. The textbook definition of an antagonist is someone or something that prevents or hinders the protagonist from reaching their goal. Could it be the villain? Of course, it could. But could it also be a friend who is getting in the way? Now you're writing interesting fiction.

In Genesis 15, Abram comes to God with his fears that he won't fulfill God's promise to one day become the father of a great generation. In verse two, Abram reminds God that he is childless and that all he has will pass down to his steward, Eliezer of Damascus. His emotions are on the table, raw doubt and fear, to which God replies, "Fear not."

As the perfect friend, God encourages Abram to stay on the path toward the goal. He squashes his fear and doubt by reminding him of God's promise to give him a son, even after Abram has been waiting for nearly fifteen years for this promise to be fulfilled. (verse4) God encourages Abram to count the innumerable stars comparing their numbers to the number of Abram's descendents. (verse 5) God speaks life into Abram. He demonstrates the character of a true friend and Abram believes him. (verse 6)

Using this template, your secondary characters, friends, and sidekicks should be there to pick your protagonist up when they fall and do whatever it takes to help them reach their goal. I think the greatest sidekick character is Samwise Gamgee, who is so dedicated to this role that he literally carries Frodo up the slopes of Mount Doom to reach his goal. I'm actually going to compare to Sam throughout this chapter because he really was so well-written and is a character worth modeling your sidekick after.

Back to Genesis 15: Like any good friend, the truth must be spoken at all costs, and God does just that. In verse 12, "a deep sleep fell upon Abram, and, lo, an horror of great darkness fell upon him." God shows Abram the burden his descendants will carry, Abram's seed, his lineage, his family. "They shall be a stranger in a land that is not theirs, and shall serve them; and they shall afflict them four hundred years." (verse13) What a terrible thing to hear! Why would God share this?

I believe he did it for two reasons. Firstly, because a good friend tells the truth at all costs. They don't sugar coat and they don't hold back to spare your feelings. They don't manipulate; they tell it how it is. Secondly, each Bible story paints a picture of redemption. As an author, we weave our own message into our books. We sometimes take our experiences and retell them through plot points apparent throughout the entire story. Would the great author, God, do it any differently? What if God is sharing his heart for humanity through this passage? Like Abram, he knew his children would fall victim to slavery (sin) and be ruled by a stranger in a strange land (the devil, Eden). Yet, he still created us, knowing his only son would lay down his life as our sacrifice (which, to drive the point home, God asks Abram to sacrifice his own only son, Isaac, but we'll get deeper into that later.) God allowed Abram to go in eyes wide open so the decision was made out of Abram's free will. This is how we, as story gods, must approach storytelling with the sons and daughters (characters) we create.

Samwise is often the voice of reason in Frodo's world, speaking the truth when no one else will; speaking the truth even when Frodo doesn't want to hear it. Likewise, Jiminy Cricket plays the truth seeking conscious to Pinocchio and Timothy Q. Mouse plays the perfect sidekick to Dumbo, speaking truth, encouragement, and forcing him to reach for the goal.

The characters influencing your protagonist

must serve their purpose well. They need to be supportive, yet truthful; selfless, yet honest. Have you created a sidekick who has the courage to speak the truth and the strength to carry the burden when the hero can't? In what ways can you show conflict and tension between them as the protagonist fights against the sidekick's good intentions? What happens when the protagonist refuses to comply?

In the next chapter, we'll take a look at Sarai, Abram's wife, to see how even a friend can become an antagonist when they interfere with the protagonist reaching their goals.

Chapter Eleven:

Friend or Foe?

To continue from the previous chapter, we will now take a look at how a secondary character can become an antagonist by thwarting the protagonist's plans to reach their goal. They don't have to be evil or a nemesis, just interfering or misleading. Let's take a look at Abram's wife, Sarai, in Genesis chapter 16.

We already know she is extraordinarily beautiful, so we can imply she uses her looks to her advantage when necessary, perhaps as a crafty and cunning woman would. Although God has promised Abram a son, Sarai twists it around and convinces her husband that it isn't through her womb from which God will give him a son, but rather her maidservant whom Sarai forces Abram to impregnate. It sounds logical. After all, Sarai is an old lady and Abram is 86 when he becomes Ishmael's dad (the maidservant's son).

But there is a fatal flaw here. This is not the

hero's journey. His path has been told to him by God, and he believes it. Through whatever sexual sorcery or logistics Sarai uses, she convinces Abram to take matters into his own hands. She becomes an antagonist.

What did this decision produce, beside an heir? Jealousy. Envy. Distrust. Anger. Rage. Hate. Of course, these are great elements to push any story along, but the emotions must be based in something; they don't just happen on their own. What caused Sarai to feel this way, to "deal hardly with" Hagar, her maidservant, and to "despise her?" (verses 5-6) It was Sarai's idea to begin with! The answer is simple: this wasn't the hero's journey. It wasn't the plan. This event took the story in a new direction in which it was never meant to go. It brought in a thread that was never intended or written in the outline.

As writers, we can utilize this story function to naturally create tension and strife in our characters. By using a trusted secondary character with good intention to logically persuade the protagonist to head in a direction that isn't on the hero's path, he will be forced to correct himself to get back on track. The secondary character will have to face the consequences of their suggestions causing tension to grow among the two characters.

Now you've created all kinds of threads with lots of possibilities. Will the two reconcile or is the relationship beyond repair? Can the hero get back on her path? What sacrifices must she make now because of this decision?

In Sarai and Abram's case, the problem really never resolves. Sarai blames Abram and asks him to punish Hagar. (verse) Abram tells Sarai that Hagar is her maidservant, so it's her problem. (verse 6) Sari beats Hagar or emotionally breaks her down to the point that she flees into the desert. (verse 6) She eventually returns home and gives birth to Ishmael, who is prophesied to be "A wild man, his hand will be against every man, and every man's hand against him; and he shall dwell in the presence of all his brethren." (verse 12)

What a horrible description of your future child. Could you imagine? "Hey, Hagar, you're gonna have the red-headed step child who nobody likes. Congratulations! It's a boy." Imagine being that kid, growing up in that environment.

I'm immediately reminded of the Dursley's and Harry Potter. A very similar tension and shunning between Harry and Dudley that is consistent in each book. Another story that brilliantly uses the altered hero's path and negative prophecy is the film *Looper*. A boy is prophesied to be the destroyer of society in the future. A man travels back in time to kill him as a boy. But our hero is supposed to kill that man when he time travels to that year. The only problem is that the hero is that man from a future story thread, and he has come back to force the hero (his younger self) on a different life path. It's an awesome story, and somehow very similar to Abram, Sarai, Hagar, and Ishmael.

As you look at the relationships between the characters in your stories, do you see opportunities for secondary characters to behave as antagonists? What problems could that cause for the hero who sidesteps his quest? What new layer of agony does the secondary character face alone? For the hero? Deepening the trauma will give depth and life to all your characters, enabling secondary characters to face their own problems, consequences, and decisions independent of the hero. When you can give true motives with genuine cause and affect results to minor characters as well as the protagonist and antagonist, you will populate your story with well-rounded, believable, breathing people that your reader may never forget. Sometimes, these characters can grow so large that they are given their own hero's quest, such as Riddick from *Pitch Black* or Logan (Wolverine) from the *X-Men* franchise.

Chapter Twelve:

Names Hold Meaning

Every word in your story should count, and any time you can utilize a word for double-meaning, it's like BINGO! God clearly shows the importance of names with meaning over and over again in the Bible. I am not a student of Hebrew, nor am I a theologian, so my observations and comments will be limited to my unschooled perspective. However, I will show what God did in Genesis chapter 17, and how you can apply it to your stories.

At 99 years old—thirteen years after the birth of Ishmael—God has a "come to Jesus moment" with Abram, reminding him of the covenant he made to "multiply thee exceedingly" and reminding Abram he would "be a father of many nations." It's interesting that God has to come down and remind him, because Abram has most likely given up on the idea of having a son with Sarai. By now, he probably believes Ishmael is the son God promised and going through

Hagar was the plan all along.

In verse 5, God says, "Neither shall they name any more be called Abram, but thy name shall be Abraham;" Why? "for a father of many nations have I made thee." Abram means "high father." Abraham means "father of many." (www.behindthenames.com) His status was about to change, so his new name reflected it.

In verse 15, God says, "As for Sarai, thy wife, thou shalt not call her Sarai, but Sarah shall her name be." Why? "And I will bless her, and give thee a son also of her, yea, I will bless her, and she shall be a mother of nations; kings of people shall be of her." (verse 16) Sarai means "quarrelsome." Sarah means "princess of the multitude." (www.shecknows.com)

How appropriate. And his reaction? "Then Abraham fell upon his face, and laughed." (verse 17) He would be 100 when the kid was born! God replies that Sarah, who also laughs in chapter 17, will bear him a son at 90 named Isaac (which means "laughter") and that Abraham's firstborn, Ishmael, (which means "God that hears") would be the father of twelve princes and a great nation, (although the covenant would pass through Isaac.) And while we're on the subject of names, Hagar means "a stranger; one that fears."

Disney is huge with names holding double-meaning. Aladdin means "faithful" in Arabic. Simba means "lion" in Swahili. Tiana means "princess" in Greek. Even when you don't know the definition, as a reader, discovering the name's meaning adds a layer to the story. You don't have to know it to enjoy the story, but by knowing it, you get a deeper understanding of the character and the author. Not to mention, these names are usually unique and memorable. Aladdin. Simba. Tiana. They are not casual, everyday names, which makes the characters easier to remember and distinguished from other characters in your story.

In my novel *Dreadlands*, I chose each character's name with purpose, based off Norse and Norwegian roots to express the personality of each one. You don't have to know the meaning to enjoy the book, but I guarantee after you know them that a new layer will draw you further into the story. Our words should always be purposed, deliberate, and provoking. If they aren't, then they are taking up space.

How can you change the names in your novel to reflect the personality of the character? What about the town or the school or corporation's name? Where can you layer the story with word meaning and definitions?

In *The Lord of the Rings*, Mordor means 'Black Land' in Sindarin and 'Land of Shadows' in Quenya. Sometimes the sounds of names works as well, like Hogwarts being a school for witches. Some characters names reflect the opposite, such as Logan in *X-Men*, which means 'Little Hollow.' I definitely think Wolverine is more fitting to his personality!

Chapter Thirteen:

Choices Have Consequences

Remember Lot, Abraham's nephew? A few chapters back, he and his uncle had split off their herds and men to part ways. Abraham let Lot choose where he would like to live first. Ringing some bells? Good. Here's the kicker: Instead of being gracious and humble by allowing his great uncle the best of the best, Lot's eyes beheld the beauty of the city Sodom, the glistening pools of water, and the greenest desert grass. His lust sent him into a place that looked good on the outside. But the grass isn't always greener....

In Genesis chapter 18, we are back with Lot to see how life's been treating him over the last few decades. "And there came two angels to Sodom at even;" (verse 1) That's awesome! Two angels have entered the city. How does Lot respond? "Behold now, my lords, turn in, I pray you into your servant's house, and tarry all night, and wash your feet, and ye shall rise up early, and go on your ways." (verse 2)

What? Lot is fervently pleading with these men to lay lo, hide, and get out before dawn. There is a huge element of fear that has entered Lot's utopian world, morphing it into a dystopian one. Sodom, the place he had imagined to be perfect, was holding a dark secret, one that caused him to fear for the safety of these angels.

Any time you can apply this to your world building and plot, the better! Creating a world that appears wonderful on the surface yet harbors something sinister or dangerous or opposing is a beautiful thing. *Invasion of the Body Snatchers. The Time Machine. The Lottery* by Shirley Jackson. By giving away small bits of information, you can create a bread trail of curiosity that your reader can't help but follow, page after page. Thomas Brown's debut novel *Lynnwood* does an excellent job of weaving the sinister throughout a sleepy town where there's always the hint that something's just not right.

In Lot's case, the men oblige, and return with him to his home for the evening. He bakes bread and makes them a feast. (verse 3) I'm sure on the outside, this reads like a normal gesture in any book, with the reader beginning to question if maybe there is something wrong with Lot; a level of paranoia rooted in his own unsubstantiated fears. Until, there comes a knock at the door. "The men of the city, even the men of Sodom, compassed the house round, both old and young, all the people from every quarter." Now, it's for real. That thing Lot was trying to prevent from happening is coming to pass. The scene has elevated slightly with this new information: there really *is* something wrong in Sodom.

Stephen King and Edgar Allen Poe are the masters of suspense-horror. They both show relatively normal people in relatively normal places who are overtaken by either an outside force or, more frequently, by their own dark heart's choices. They show the "what if's" when a person receives exactly what they *think* they want or need. *Thinner. The Tell-Tale Heart. The Monkey's Paw,* another great example by author W.W. Jacobs.

Lot is in the midst of the consequences from his own dark heart's choices. He is harboring two angels, messengers of God, who the men of Sodom want brought out of Lot's home so that they might gang rape them. Seriously. Hey, it's right there in verse 5 if you don't believe me. Nothing new under the sun, remember? The Old Testament isn't some collection of wishy-washy bedtime stories about old men with long grey beards who manage floating zoos, or beat up giants with pebbles and then write poetry about it. It is filled with every joy and treacherous act mankind is capable of, and if it were written today, it would most likely be on the banned book list.

Lot refuses to release the angels to the crowd, offering instead his two virgin daughters to take their place. (verse 8) This is a desperate man who is deep in the refuse of his own poor judgment and lustful choices. Can you imagine? But this action, this offering, is actually a sign that he is trying to do the right thing. Lot knows these men are on God's mission, and while I'm sure he loves his daughters, his decision to substitute them in the angels stead shows he is reprioritizing and refocusing. No longer driven by his own selfish desires, Lot is genuinely trying to do what is pleasing in God's sight.

But is it too late?

God honors his willingness, an attribute God repeats constantly throughout the Bible. Genesis 19:11, "And they (the angels) smote the men that were at the door of the house with blindness, both small and great, so that they wearied themselves to find the door."

Now the race is on. With the men of the city blinded, Lot is told to gather his wife and daughters and to leave Sodom before God destroys it. "And when the morning arose, then the Angels hastened Lot, saying, Arise, take thy wife, and thy two daughters, which are here; lest thou be consumed in the iniquity of the city." (verse 15) But Lot lingers. Why? Have you ever made a mistake? Have you ever lost everything because of it? Have you ever had to return to someone you truly wronged to ask for forgiveness? That's why. Those are hard consequences to face. But they make terrific plot points!

If you can position your characters to where their choices lead them to make fatal mistakes that cost them everything, and force them to repent to those they've wronged, you've got a base for great tension and an opportunity to show the dark heart choices of humanity that your readers can relate to. We don't like to admit it, but we would all agree that sin is in us. As the clock ticks and time runs out, Lot is dragged out of Sodom along with his wife and two of his daughters (the others stayed behind with their unbelieving husbands) by the angels. They are instructed to

"Escape for they life; look not behind thee, neither stay thou in all the plain (where Abraham lives); escape to the mountain, lest thou be consumed." (verse 17)

So here's a broken man. He entered Sodom, the best of the best, with so many servants, flocks, and herds that he had to separate them from his uncle's. He leaves Sodom with two of his daughters and his wife, who ends up turning into a pillar of salt when she disobeys and looks back at Sodom's destruction.

In the end, "the Lord rained upon Sodom and upon Gomorrah brimstone and fire from the Lord out of Heaven." (verse 24) But God remembered his promise to Abraham and kept Lot safe (see Genesis 18:20-33)

In your story, have you allowed your characters to make decisions that appear good, but carry weighty consequences? How can you expand those to ripple out even further in their lives? Into the lives of those around them? By allowing your characters to give into their own dark heart desires, you can create a natural set of consequences that will shake their world and bring it all crashing to the ground. Then, with the now humble character, you can help rebuild their life and their world into something great, like Ebenezer Scrooge from Dicken's *A Christmas Carol* or Katniss Everdeen from the *Hunger Games*.

Chapter Fourteen:

Real Life Ain't Fair

Abraham and Sarah are traveling to a new country. They arrive, and Abraham tells the king that Sarah is his sister (Genesis 20:2), a truth because they share the same father (déjà vu?). He fears they will kill him because of her beauty. Seriously? It was bad enough when Abraham pulled this stunt back in Genesis 2 when Sarah was in her sixties. Here she is in her nineties, and it's happening again? Nonetheless, the king does take her in and Abraham's life is spared.

"But God came to Abimelech in a dream by night, and said to him, Behold, thou are but a dead man, for the woman which though hast taken; for she is a man's wife." Genesis 20:3 This king is in big trouble. He was lied to, yet his head is on the line. When God says, "You're a dead man," that's a case closed in my book. King Abimelech pleads his case anyway: "We're a righteous nation," "the husband and wife lied," and "It was an accident."

Of course, God allows him a pardon if he restores Sarah to Abraham, which Abimelech does. But he speaks his mind in verse 9. "Then Abimelech called Abraham and said unto him, What hast thou done unto us? And what have I offended thee that though hast brought on me and on my kingdom a great sin? Though hast done deeds unto me that ought not to be done."

We know the answer: Abraham was afraid for his life, and this tactic had worked for him just fine in the past. He defends that he hadn't really lied, since they were technically brother and sister, but the wrong had already happened. The king showers him with sheep and oxen and servants and 1,000 pieces of silver. He hadn't done anything wrong, really...he was the victim of circumstance. But he still had to pay.

Real life ain't fair.

Let's look at this from another angle. Let's compare Abraham's plight to Lot's. Both entered foreign kingdoms with their families to make a new home, although Lot selfishly chose the better portion leaving Abraham the rest. Both faced confrontation for their choices, although Abraham was found blameless for lying and Lot was found blameless for trying. Both lost their wives, except Sarah was returned. Technically, Lot was trying to do the right thing and lost everything, while Abraham was looking out for himself and received an abundance in return. Why?

Real life ain't fair.

Your story is a reflection of real life. Why is everything working out so easily? How come your main character just knows that important piece of information? Why is it that every plan is perfectly executed with everything she needs in her grasp. It's not real life.

When Rue dies in the *Hunger Games*, my inner

self screams, "That's not fair!" Yet I knew she was dead the first time she was introduced in the story. The same happens when Ender Wiggins learns that he wasn't playing a game, but that he had actually exterminated an entire species. These stories are so powerful because they take into account the fact that real life ain't fair, and bad things happen to people with good intentions.

Let's take a look at one more example. At the end of Genesis 19:30-38, after Lot has left Sodom, lost everything—including his wife—he is living in a cave with his two daughters. He's drunk on wine all the time, drowning in his misery and loss. His young daughters (whom he had offered to the mob for them to gang rape in lieu of sodomizing the two angels) are alone with him. I can't imagine how they felt. They'd lost everything too, including the care and protection of their father.

So dad's drunk, and the girls take turns having intercourse with him so they can both become pregnant. Hey, you can take the girl out of Sodom, but you can't take Sodom out of the girl! Needless to say, two boys are born, simultaneously brothers and cousins. Talk about dysfunction.

What's the point? Real life ain't fair, and our choices have consequences that ripple and grow and take on lives of their own, sometimes even after we try doing the right thing. My mind instantly goes to Obi Wan Kenobi and Anakin Skywalker. Obi Wan is desperate to teach Anakin the way of the Jedi, knowing he will restore order to the Force. But in the end, Anakin joins Lord Sidious on the Dark Side. Obi Wan did everything right, yet it wasn't enough.

Broken-hearted, he loses not just his padawan, but a friend he found to be more like a brother. Why? Say it with me: real life ain't fair. So, your story shouldn't be fair either.

In what areas of your manuscript can you adjust the balance and create more realism? How can you make it harder for your characters to succeed? Where can you bring in the powerlessness that your characters have done what's right, yet still failed? In what way can you make your story world reflect the real world? Want a good study example? Read the entire *Maze Runner* series. Talk about unfair!

Real life ain't fair, so let's shake things up in our stories' reality.

Chapter Fifteen:

The Prophecy Fulfilled

Many stories center around the prophesied one, the great prophecy, in which usually unexplainable and unbelievable circumstances produce a savior, no matter how awkward or un-heroic he or she appears. Harry Potter. Luke Skywalker. Gregor the Overlander. Percy Jackson. Clark Kent. The list goes on.

In Genesis chapter 21, we are introduced to this amazing experience through the long awaited (fifteen years!) pregnancy of Sarah by Abraham and the birth of their promised son, Isaac: the prophecy fulfilled.

At one-hundred years old, Abraham becomes a father for the second time, and at ninety, beautiful Sarah births and nurses her miracle son. This child is destined to be the first of many, the first seed to grow and produce a great nation.

Do you think he popped out of the womb with all the grace and wisdom to handle the task set out before him? Did he enter the world fully grasping his place and purpose? Imagine Sarah kneading bread with young Isaac in the kitchen, reminding him that some day he would father a great nation. Or Abraham with teenage Isaac resting in the shade of a tree for lunch, talking about the great responsibility God had entrusted to him as his birthright.

I can picture other days, too, when Isaac disobeyed or reacted through puberty or did stupid things that kids do. Abraham and Sarah must have whispered their fears and disbelief over their pillows on those nights wondering if Isaac would ever become the man God intended, doubting they were equipped for the great task God had charged them with.

I think of Peter Parker and Uncle Ben: "With great power comes great responsibility." But Peter doesn't want the gift. He wants a normal life with Mary Jane, one that is not possible for Spiderman. And Harry Potter, who has spent his entire life in the dark about the world of magic, but is suddenly thrust into an environment where he is expected to be the greatest wizard of all time.

The greatest part of the prophecy fulfilled story is the hero's journey. Her growth as she doubts herself, denies her gifts, refuses her task, and ignores the needs of the people that only she can fulfill. It's an awesome and powerful experience that brings the reader alongside the hero to feel their own self-doubt and inabilities and fears as they, too, discover inner strength, perseverance, and sacrifice for the prophecy's fulfillment.

Whether or not you're writing a story with a prophecy, take some time to study books or movies that are based around this element. What emotions were stirred up in you? How did the author accomplish this? Can you diagram the hero's ups and downs? What inner and outer forces contributed to their growth and fall-backs?

As a prophecy is fulfilled and a hero is born, so the same exact environment and circumstances work to create a nemesis, an idea which will be explored in the next chapter.

Chapter Sixteen:

The Nemesis

Sarah has singlehandedly created a huge mess. Sure, Abraham went along with it and created a son with Sarah's maidservant, but I seriously doubt he would have come to that decision on his own. (Sounds a bit like Eve and Adam, doesn't it?) Now we throw Isaac in the mix and things go from bad to nemesis.

In Genesis 21:9, it says, "And Sarah saw the son of Hagar the Egyptian, which she had born unto Abraham, mocking." If you remember back to the chapter when Sarah beat Hagar and sent her into the wilderness to die, she returned with Ishmael, a broken woman. I doubt she would be mocking Sarah here. Have you ever thought someone was talking about you when they weren't? Or misinterpreted what they said or their motives? I'm thinking that's more than likely what happened here.

Those are great idiosyncrasies to build into your characters. According to Dr. Albert Mehrabian, 93%

of all communication is non-verbal (www.nonverbalgroup.com). That means 7% of communication comes from the actual dialogue. Your characters should be filled with gestures, facial expressions, sarcasm, vocal tones, posture, etc. Do your characters convey exactly what they feel at all time? Do they lie, stretch the truth, soften the blow, or constrict around certain characters and relax around others. These are real life physiological responses and choices. Whether on purpose or reactionary that must be in your books if you want your characters to move from two-dimensional to three-dimensional. *The Emotion Thesaurus* by Angela Ackerman and Becca Puglisis is an excellent resource of mental and physical responses to emotions.

This is what I think is happening to Sarah at this moment. Her own impatience and distrust of God caused this whole ordeal to begin with. Now that the prophetic son has been born, (a foreshadow to many more to come, leading ultimately to the birth of Jesus) she tells Abraham to "Cast out this bondwoman and her son: for the son of this bondwoman shall not be heir with my son, even with Isaac." (verse 10)

Sarah has basically become the evil stepmother because, like it or not, Ishmael is technically her step-son. And what a horrible burden to place on Abraham: kick out your bastard kid and his mother or I'm taking Isaac and moving in with my mother.

This is a great, often used plot line. Cinderella is the most obvious example, but variations of this plot can be seen even in the relationship between Harry Potter and the Dursleys or *The Man in the Iron Mask*.

Luckily, God intervenes and comforts Abraham

by telling him not to grieve, but to listen to his wife "for in Isaac shall thy seed be called." (verse 12) But that's not all. Verse 13 continues: "And also of the son of the bondwoman will I make a nation because he is thy seed."

God keeps his promises, and both boys eventually grew into men who fathered great nations, and twelve tribes. Isaac fathered the Israelites, the Hebrew's, today's Jewish nation. Ishmael fathered his nations through an Egyptian wife, which today inhabit the nations of Lebanon, Syria, Turkey, Iraq, Saudi Arabia, Yemen, United Arab-Emirates, Jordan, Egypt, Libya, Sudan, Morocco, Tunisia, and the pseudo-nation Palestine. (www.bibletools.org) These nations consist mainly of people who do not wish for Israel to exist.

I wonder if the root of Ishmael's heart toward Isaac still feeds this hatred through his descendants toward God's chosen people, according to the Scriptures. I wonder also if Sarah had only been patient and faithful, not intervening in God's plans, would there be turmoil today in the Middle East. We will never know.

These are great tools to apply to your writing. Having deep, common bonds between the hero and the nemesis make their conflict that much greater. Using an outside force or character to force the separation makes the problem grow and the emotions deepen between the hero and the villain. Superman and Zod; Harry Potter and Voldemort; Thomas and WICKED. These relationships both attract and repel simultaneously because of the bonds between and similarities of the two characters, helping to highlight

their differences and shape them into those figures we
can't forget, long after we've read "The End."

Chapter Seventeen:

Parallels

Genesis chapter 22 is one of my favorite Bible stories. This is where Abraham is told to sacrifice Isaac. "Take now thy son, thine only son Isaac, whom thou lovest, and get thee into the land of Moriah; and offer him there for a burnt offering upon one of the mountains which I will tell thee of." (verse 2)

This is so powerful. As a mother, I couldn't begin to imagine what that must have felt like, although I'm pretty sure I would NOT have handled it in the same manner as Abraham. I'd have gone kicking and screaming filled with bitterness and anger, if I even went at all. Most likely, I'd have pulled a Jonah here. (we'll save that story for a different book.)

So Abraham, who was totally fine being childless "Abram," is promised a son. His wife rushes God by giving Hagar to Abram and Ishmael is born. Then, the promised son Isaac is delivered and

Abraham is forced to banish Hagar and Ishmael. Now, God is asking him to kill Isaac and return back to the beginning: a childless Abram, only this time full of heartache over his many losses.

But that isn't how the story goes, is it?

Verse 3 tells how Abraham rose early with two of his men and Isaac, and with wood for the burn offering and began their journey. Verse 4 explains that on the third day, Abraham laid his eyes upon the spot where God was leading him. Verse 5 shows Abraham telling his helpers to stay while he and Isaac went to worship, until they both returned (since Abraham believed God would provide a lamb to replace his son). In verse 6, "Abraham took the wood of the burnt offering, and laid it upon Isaac his son." Verse 7 has Isaac getting nervous, asking his father about the lamb, to which Abraham replies in verse 8 that God would provide. Verses 9-12 shows Isaac laid upon the alter, Abraham's hands lifting the knife, and the intervention by the Angel of the Lord commanding Abraham to stop; telling Abraham he has proved worthy and passed the test. Verse 13 provides a ram, caught in a thicket by its horns, to be the sacrifice in Isaac's stead.

What a story!

By itself, we can learn so much about creating tension and conflict in our writing. The power of love and trust. Fear and faith coexisting. But I'd like to use this story to illustrate the technique of parallels in story.

To me, when I can show a mini version of a climactic event early in the story, it layers the plot and makes the climax that much more powerful. The reader feels like they have a vested interest. Will it turn out the same this time—will Luke Skywalker make the same choice as Anakin? Or will the character have grown enough to see their follies and make the right decision—can Marty McFly overcome his insecurities when he's called a chicken and change his future?

In the Bible, this story parallels the story of Jesus remarkably. Let's break it down:

- Both Isaac and Jesus are their father's beloved only sons
- Both are fulfillments of prophecy
- Both are expected to be the sacrificial lamb
- Both have fathers willing to lay their sons on the alter
- Both were "dead" until the third day of redemption (Isaac in future tense expectation, Jesus in literal form)
- Both carried the very wood upon which they would be sacrificed
- Both stories include thorns on the head of the sacrifice

Finding ways to parallel events in your story is not difficult. Sometimes, you do it on purpose: most times, similarities jump out at you during editing. When you see minor parallels you've accidentally built in, your job becomes highlighting them or bringing them out more—but not too much—for the reader to have a string of dots to connect. It can be subtle, like Frodo becoming more and more like Gollum under the ring's power or it can be the pivotal point in the story, like Harry Potter and Voldemort's connection, event unto death (ex. Wand cores from the same phoenix feathers, both orphans, Voldemort fears death so much he separates his soul into many pieces while Harry constantly faces death and eventually willingly enters it).

Where have you established parallels in your story that could be drawn bolder? Are your protagonist and antagonist on similar paths? How can you show one make a decision toward destruction while the other, faced with the same circumstances, chooses life? Building in these "aha" moments will build a following of readers who can't wait for you to release your next book, which is, after all, what most authors are hoping for.

Chapter Eighteen:

Rules

We all have them in our lives: rituals, customs, laws, and the lure surrounding them. They govern our decisions and our families, our instincts, even our dreams. No greater element of realism can bring depth and dimension to your story than the rules. And I'm not just talking science fiction or fantasy.

In Genesis 23, Sarah dies at the age of 127. Abraham was 137 and Isaac was 37. They were sojourners in a land they did not belong in, with a people they did not belong to. Abraham wept and mourned for Sarah, (verse 2) but then "And Abraham stood up from before his dead, and spoke unto the sons of Heth, saying, I am a stranger and sojourner with you: give me a possession of a burying place with you, that I may bury my dead out of my sight." (verse 3-4)

So he wants a piece of land to call his own in which to bury Sarah. But that's not all. The people remind Abraham of his status as a prince among them, offering him choice picks of the sepulchers, even offering their own personal sepulchers free of charge. Grave plots and headstones are expensive, let alone the nicest, most adorned, worthy-of-a-prince sepulchers.

But Abraham had not been brought up that way. His people buried their dead outside the camp; outside the city. He bows and reminds them of this before he asks to speak with their leader regarding a particular piece of property: the cave of Machpelah (defined as "portion" at www.biblestudytool.com) located at the end of the field belonging to Ephron, son of Zohar. Abraham wants to pay face value for the cave.

Why? His honor, reputation, and dignity were on the line. What sort of man doesn't buy his wife's bones an eternal resting place? His cultural standing wouldn't allow it, and he and Ephron barter back and forth until Ephron quotes him the fair market value of 400 shekels of silver or approximately $41,500 US Dollars. (verses 10-15) Finally, in front of all the people as his witness, Abraham purchases the cave for a burial place for Sarah and eventually, for himself and Isaac.

Strong convictions of belief and ritual created this entire chapter in Genesis. So how important are rituals, customs, laws, and lure in stories? They provide the world in which our characters will follow or fight. The Civil Wars in the *Hunger Games* led to the formation of Panem under the Capital, and the distinctions of the districts. The Formic Wars that caused the near extinction of Earth led to the recruit and training of children to battle an alien species under the guise of a game; the world that Ender Wiggins was born in. The rules of *Twilight* were slightly different than those of traditional vampire lure, giving the story world a fresh approach to a classic monster. And the rules and lure of Hogwarts were so spectacular it was built in real life, to be experienced by the five sense.

What customs and laws have you created for your story world? How deep does the lure run? Have you constructed a unique lure with rules that force the characters to comply or rebel? Can you take current lure and tweak it to be your own?

Constructing a deep rooted story world with rituals, customs, laws, and lure will keep your story from toppling over; as with a tree, the larger the trunk and boughs, the greater depth and reach and hold the root system must contain.

Chapter Nineteen:

Plotting Coincidence

Sometimes, truth is stranger than fiction.

I hear stories or watch events unfold and say to myself, "If I wrote that in a book, no one would believe it." Yet life is filled with bizarre coincidence, strange similarities, and predetermined paths. How can we learn to build believable predictions within our story worlds? How can we mimic life's invariable ebb and flow by plotting coincidence? Let's study Genesis 24 and see how the great Author did it.

Abraham is very old and near death. He is living among the Canaanites and begs his servant to swear an oath that he will not allow Isaac to choose a wife among the ungodly women, but will journey "unto my (Abraham's) country, and to my kindred, and take a wife unto my son Isaac." (verse 4) The servant asks what he should do if the woman refuses to come, and Abraham tells him that God will send an Angel to bring forth the wife He has chosen for Isaac.

He also states that if the woman still won't come, the servant will be clear of the oath.

So the scene is set: an angel will bring forth the perfect woman who is willing to blindly leave her family to marry a man she has never met. Okay. And this servant must swear an oath to Abraham that he will make this happen. Totally believable. Not!

The servant binds himself to the oath and leaves with ten camels carrying supplies and gifts headed to Mesopotamia, the City of Nahor, the country of Abraham's kin. In this day and age, the women went out in the evening to draw water from the well. The servant arrived prior to this and led his camels to kneel to rest. Imagine his anxiety. How would he know which was the woman the Angel had chosen? What if he couldn't find her? How could he ever return home without fulfilling his oath?

On a side note, these are the kinds of probing questions, by the way, your characters should ask themselves to show their inner struggles. Then narrative should show these questions as the characters thoughts are shown on paper. Without getting inside the characters head, and simply moving from plot point to plot point, you are creating nothing different than a movie can show (in much less time). These moments connect the reader to your characters. They allow the reader to draw upon their own emotions through empathy or through their perceived emotions and sympathy to actually care about your characters.

Back to the story: to resolve these inconsistencies, the servant prays in his heart, "And let it come to pass, that the damsel to whom I shall say, Let down they pitcher, I pray thee, that I may drink;

and she shall say, Drink, and I will give thy camels drink also; let the same be she that thou hast appointed for thy servant Isaac." (verse 4) A simple enough request. Rationally, as a writer, I would feel the story would be way too contrived if the answer came about exactly as the servant requested. I mean who would believe that? But verses 15-21 do just that. Rebecca arrives immediately to draw water, offers some to the servant, and draws more for the camels. And you know what? It works. It not only works, but if fits like a puzzle, totally believable.

But the coincidence doesn't stop there. Oh, no. Rebecca is not just the-girl-who-draws-water-for-the-camels-too, she is also the daughter of Abraham's brother, Nahor, making her Isaac's cousin (which was okay back then). Not only is this woman a relative, she is a direct descendant of Abraham's blood, another remarkable (yet somehow totally believable) coincidence.

The remainder of the chapter is the servants retelling to Rebecca's family of Abraham's status, his oath, the servant's prayer, and the fulfillment of it all in Rebecca's actions. What an incredible coincidence, you say? No one in this group batted an eye. No snide remarks or request for proof. Just acceptance of the great coincidence.

Does this obvious tactic work in other works of literature?

When Harry Potter needed to learn more about Nicholas Flammel and lacked a way into the restricted area of the library, did the appearance of the invisibility cloak feel like a far fetched coincidence? Or perfect timing.

When Katniss was stuck in a tree with tributes sleeping at the base, was it a contrived addition to have not only Rue appear but her to show Katniss the tracker jacker hive that just so happened to be hanging off the branch right above her? Or was it the handiwork of a crafty author who expertly manifested coincidence out of thin air?

The trick with bringing believable coincidence into a story is to state or show it before you need it, not after. For example, if we had never seen Katniss shoot an arrow or hunt or forage or trap, it would be an awfully unbelievable coincidence to suddenly see her exhibit these behaviors in the Hunger Games. And if we never saw Ender as an expert problem solver and true leader, it would be hard to swallow when he outwits the adults and ends their war.

Have you shown your characters solving their problems with convenient coincidences or have you taken the time to plot them into believable situations? Where have you written in set-ups, but never followed through with delivery?

Coincidences happen every day and people naturally connect the dots to arrive at end results to force order into their lives. By building in bread trails as story threads, you will add layers of believability to your characters and story world by leading to coincidences that don't just make sense, they make fact of your fiction.

Chapter Twenty:

Play-Rewind-Repeat

Who doesn't love a story with some good sibling rivalry? It's all over the Bible, starting with Cain and Abel, Isaac and Ishmael, and now in Genesis 25 with the birth of Jacob and Esau. It's interesting to see how often God show the sins of the father becoming the sins of his children. So often, they are repeated from generation to generation. Adam blamed Eve and God for his sins, then Cain blamed Able and God for his sins. Isaac and his brother are enemies because of birthright as a result of the devious interfering plans of their mothers and Jacob and Esau do more of the same, as discussed in another chapter. Abraham lies about his wife being his sister out of fear due to her insurmountable beauty, and son Isaac does the same with Rebecca in Genesis 26:7.

On a side note to becoming a better writer, I think these repetitive themes and actions cannot be ignored. They are universal and powerful and dark and deep. They are the side of good that rises to the surface when life is heated up. They reveal character. Unchecked, these sins are passed down to the next generation, something I believe God strongly wanted to convey through the lives of the patriarchs. They are a warning of what our lives can become if we are not careful and aware of the generational consequences of our choices.

As writers, it is our privilege to mimic the world around us but with the power to make things right again; to bring balance to the Universe by "the end"; to restore order in a chaotic life. These scriptural techniques of characters doing things because of generational predetermination or genetic cursing is extremely powerful. It's the lifeline behind *A Christmas Carol*, the greatest fear in Ender Wiggins's heart, and the essence of Harry Potter's quest to not just defeat, but understand Voldemort. Folly repeating folly is real life, but folly overcoming folly is the magic of storytelling.

In Genesis 25, we are introduced to Jacob and Esau, the sons of Isaac and Rebecca. Abraham has passed (but not before remarrying and having six more sons!) giving all that he has to Isaac. (verse 5) At 175 years old, he is gathered to his people. Here's the verse that jumped out at me: "And his sons Isaac and Ishmael buried him in the cave of Machpelah; in the field of Ephron the son of Zohar the Hittite," (verse 9)

Imagine that scene. Both brothers are tasked to bury their father, the firstborn and the beloved. They were both fully aware that Ishmael had been cast from his home on account of Isaac's birth. They were both aware that Abraham gave all that he had to Isaac.

Think of the tension! Isaac is 75 years old and Ishmael is 88. In our society, that's a lifetime. Has Ishmael hated Isaac his whole life? Has Isaac carried guilt over the incident all those years? It's interesting to consider the emotions in this scene that go unexpressed in the text. I wonder if Ishmael cried or if he had serious daddy issues. These two men do not reconcile or forgive, according to the scripture. They simply do what is required of them and bury their father as custom dictates.

Fast forward to the pregnancy of Rebecca, Isaac's wife. Two brothers are in her womb. Two nations, as with Isaac and Ishmael, who both fathered twelve tribes; one to become the nations and the other **the** nation. Verse 23 continues: "and two manner of people shall be separated from thy bowels; and the one people shall be stronger than the other people; and the elder shall serve the younger."

Rewind-Play-Repeat.

And so, Esau appeared first, "red all over like a hairy garment," (verse 25) followed by his brother, "and his hand took hold on Esau's heels; and his name was called Jacob," (verse 26) (To accentuate the point of an earlier chapter Esau means "hairy" and Jacob means "supplanter" defined as: one who takes or attempts to take the rightful place of another (vocabulary.com). To demonstrate the chapter even further, Jacob's name is changed to Israel, which will be covered later.)

Esau was a cunning hunter while Jacob was a tent dweller, like many of the patriarchs before him. Isaac loved Esau because he cooked venison, but Rebecca loved Jacob most. Again, two brothers who were played against each other by favoritism. But honestly, Esau was a man consumed by emotion and the pleasures of the flesh. One day, he came in from hunting to the smell of Jacob's home cooking. "I'm starved," Esau said. "Give me some." "Only if you give me your birthright," Jacob quipped. "Fine. Take it. What good is it to me if I die of starvation."

And a deal is struck.

Jacob gave up his birthright, or the rights and privileges entitled to him for being the firstborn, in exchange for a bowl of lentils and some bread. Perhaps not the greatest choice he could've made, and not the characteristics of a leader. Esau valued the hunt, the meat, spending time to become a great hunter. He lost sight of his birthright by over-valuing his need for food. Jacob tended flocks and herds. He was familiar with the importance of knowing where his animals were at all times. He was a homebody, loving his family, and not wild like his brother.

How can we apply the lessons from this chapter to our writing? Let's start by finding places where our characters are faced with identical choices to those in their past or in the past of someone they are close to. How can you show tension in this moment? Will he take the familiar, easy path or the unknown road toward redemption and rebirth? Have you shown her inner struggle as she tries not to become what she fears she is destined to be? What about those fears to be who the world expects her to be although she feels unequipped for the challenge?

In life, we often find that we repeat the same mistakes several times before we get it right. Maybe it's a family curse, like in *Holes*, that has been put on our shoulders to make right. More likely it's the younger version of ourselves swearing we will never grow up and become like this person or that person in their lives, only to find out that we have. It isn't easy to overcome these flaws, these curses, and many of us are never able to achieve that level of success. But in our story world, where we are guaranteed the ability to restore order, these flaws and innate hurdles are just the traits our budding heroes need to grow into the saviors of our books.

Chapter Twenty-One:

Trust Through Blind Faith

Genesis chapter 26 is about making new out of old. The entire portion focuses on re-digging old wells and the digging of new ones. "And there was a famine in the land," (verse1) Famine means no water. No water means no life. Not for the people, not for the animals, not for the earth. It's a time when people need to come together to share resources, but also a time when evil people exploit the need for basic needs. This chapter was challenging to find a lesson in. I kept digging my own wells till I discovered the concepts of dependency and blind trust.

In verse two, Isaac journeys from his home in The Negev (between Kadesh and Bered, about 50 miles south of Beersheba) to King Abimelech into Gerar. The Lord appears before Isaac and says, "Go not down to Egypt; dwell in the land which I shall tell thee of:" Back in the day, Egypt was a hub for civilization. We're talking 2,000 BCE, the Fertile

Crescent, the rule of Babylon. So here God tells Isaac not to go to the land where he will surely find essentials and survival, but to stay in Gerar with the Philistines. Does Isaac immediately unpack and get settled? Not so much. In verses 3-4, it sounds like God is pleading his case, reminding Isaac of the promise he made Abraham, which would be fulfilled in his seed multiplied "as the stars of heaven." (verse 2)

Isaac would have to put two and two together to realize if God was leading him somewhere besides Egypt, and remembering His promise, then Isaac and his family would survive. God was guaranteeing his safety. But it isn't until the clincher, verse 5, that Isaac agrees to stay. "Because that Abraham obeyed my voice and kept my charge, my commandments, my statutes, and my laws." His obedience was his saving grace and the source of his blessings. Interestingly, the author does not give an account of how much time passed between the initial famine and the request of God till verse 6, "And Isaac dwelt in Gerar."

So after a year, Isaac had increased his worth 100-fold from what he had sown in the land and the Philistines envied his wealth, his servants, his flocks, and his herds. "And King Abimelech said unto Isaac, Go from us; for though art much mightier than we."

Wait a minute. Hadn't God told him to stay here? Only to get thrown out?

But Isaac complied, pitched his tents in the valley, and re-dug all of his father's wells that the Philistines had filled with dirt after Abraham's death. Then, the herdsmen of the valley claimed the wells belonged to them; Isaac's men dug another well, only to lose it to the herdsmen of Gerar. I doubt this was part of his expectations when he agreed to trust God with blind faith. Still, he dug another well and the herdsmen left him alone. I'd be feeling extremely discouraged by this point. But Isaac is visited by God and reminded him that his seed will multiply and be blessed. So he pitches his tents and digs a new well.

Then, Abimelech and his closest friend and the chief captain of his army come to Isaac to beg his forgiveness, forming an oath between them. "And they said, We saw certainly that the Lord was with thee." (verse 28)

I'm reminded of two characters right away who fit the mold of this story: Frodo Baggins and Harry Potter. Both are thrust into situations that are much greater than they had originally been told or thought. Both are constantly reminded of the great task that has been burdened to them. Both are betrayed by those they were expected to depend upon. Both place trust through blind faith on the world and direction given to them by a great father figure with substantial supernatural powers.

Can you find places in your own writing where your characters trust through blind faith only to be led into places that make it seem like they've made the wrong decision? How can you increase the tension through the betrayal of others? Did you include a steadfast character to remind the hero of his journey and to encourage him to stay on the path? Are there highly respected authority figures who are larger than life guarding the character along their quest?

It's a very scary and unguarded feeling to trust with blind faith, but it gives such depth to your characters, and it really gives the reader a vested emotional interest in the outcome. When it seems unfair, we get angry and demand justice. And when justice comes by "the end" in whatever form the writer sees fit, we feel satisfied as a reader that order has been restored to the universe once again, if only for a short while.

Chapter Twenty-Two:

Trickery & Betrayal

Betrayal is a powerful technique to use as an author, and what better chapter topic to follow one on *Trust & Blind Faith* then *Trickery & Betrayal*. It's my sick sense of humor, I suppose. Betrayal in life can be a deal breaker, one of those things you may never recover from. And when it's performed through trickery, the wound can stay opened forever.

In Genesis 27, Isaac is dying. His eyes have dimmed with blindness from old age and as he lies on his deathbed, he requests his final meal. He calls in his eldest son, Esau, to bestow upon him the father's blessing, or the wealth of the father. He asks his son to hunt a deer and cook its meat the way Isaac loves it, affirming his son's inner need for acceptance by "performance" defining "place" and Esau is on his way. As opposed to the birthright, which Esau already gave to Jacob—consisting of the right, privilege, or possession entitled by birth or the status of the head of the household and the right to inherit the estate of the father—the blessing was more of a last will and testament, and was usually prized as the revealing of God's will in the son's life. This could be given to anyone, but was often reserved in its greatest abundance for the firstborn.

Let me stop here. Do you see how greatly established the rules of this culture are ingrained into society? Have you taken the time to cultivate deep-rooted cultural rules into your story world?

Back to Genesis 27: "And Rebecca heard when Isaac spake to Esau her son." (verse 5) Enter the treachery and the cunning, scene one, stage right. While Esau is out in the field hunting, Rebecca pulls Jacob aside. "Dad's about to hit the Highway to Purgatory and is bless your brother. But that ain't happening. Go grab a goat, I'll cook it the way Dad likes, and he'll bless you. Easy-peasy."

But Jacob doesn't latch on so quickly. "Esau my brother is a hairy man, and I am a smooth man:" (verse 11) No problem. Rebecca just covers his skin with animal fur since Dad is as blind as a bat anyway. But Jacob fears the curse that will follow should his dad realize the degree of this trickery. So Mom takes any curse upon herself.

A deal is struck.

Again, the power of words in this society was tremendously impactful. Stemming back to Genesis 1, when God *said* let there be light. It makes me wonder why I don't watch what I say more carefully. But I digress.

So everything goes as planned. Jacob tricks his father and receives the blessing. Esau shows up soon after with his father's stew only to learn he is too late; the blessing is gone. There is nothing left. Interestingly, that means there was no plan to bless Jacob with anything, for it was all going to Esau. Maybe Rebecca knew this. Maybe not. Either way, when Esau discovers the degree of the betrayal through trickery, "he cried with a great and exceeding bitter cry," (verse 34) Remember, his name was Jacob, the supplanter? Here, in verse 36, Esau brings that up again, although he's in pity party mode, stating that Jacob took away his birthright when Esau actually gave it freely. Rose-colored glasses and a rearview mirror can do that to reality.

Remember that when you are showing your characters reacting to the consequences of their folly from their own poor decisions. Most of the time, people blame shift, finger point, and excuse themselves to the point that their physical memory of an event is altered and they remember it differently. Think about that human shortcoming as you create round, believable characters.

The result is that Esau hated Jacob and in his heart; he vowed to kill him after the days of his father's mourning had passed. (verse 41) Of course, Rebecca overheard these things and sent Jacob back to her hometown, to Uncle Labin's, until Esau's anger cooled. (verses 43-44)

Funny how he gained everything: the land, the servants who worked it, the wealth, the animals; yet Jacob left with only the clothes on his back to flee from his brother's wrath. I wonder how well that plan worked out for him.

My favorite TV series is called "Supernatural."

And yes, while it's driven by monsters and demons, angels and hunters, at its core, it is the story of two brothers who love each other. They protect each other, lie to each other, die for each other, hate each other, but always come back to square one: all they've got in this world is each other. It truly is the driving force behind the show.

What ways can you deliver believable trickery and betrayal into your stories? Subtlety works well. Keeping the reader in the dark alongside the protagonist is great, like Katniss in *Catching Fire* and Harry Potter at the end of the series with Snape and Dumbledore. It's also effective to show the truth in treachery to the reader who can watch helplessly with a broken heart while the betrayal is revealed, like Obi-Won with Anakin Skywalker in *Revenge of the Sith* or the old hag who's really the wicked queen in *Snow White*. Remember to always show the price the character must pay in exchange for their betrayal. If there is no cost, there is no stake. If there's nothing at stake, your reader won't care.

In your story, where have you let people off too easy? Have you set up moments of trickery and betrayal? Did the audience know in advance or was it revealed to them at the same time as the main character? Why? How much does the reveal affect the emotional impact to both MC and reader?

Trickery and betrayal happen in every day life from tiny decisions that may go unnoticed (revealing the true heart of your character and foreshadowing a greater deceit to come) to major events that alter lives, relationships, and even the future of the universe in one way or another. The degree to which you incorporate the treachery into your story will make it more believable and the resulting anger, hatred, and even vengeance to kill in exchange for the deceit will bring depth and heartache to an otherwise perfect story world.

Chapter Twenty-Three:

Showing Inner Struggles

There are basically two types of people in the world and they are labeled as glass half full or half empty. Some people go through life seeing all its potential, taking the bull by the horns, and making lemonade from lemons. Others flounder from feeling to feeling, seeing life as the result of events strung together, riding a rollercoaster of ups and downs, and taking life's lemons and sucking on them until their teeth hurt.

We all have problems. Everyone from the richest to the poorest, from the healthiest to the sickest, to the young and old alike. The issue isn't the "have", it's the "how."

How do you handle life when it isn't fair?

How do you handle people when they aren't fair?

How do you handle *you* when things don't go your way?

It's fascinating to compare the personalities of Jacob and Esau. If you recall, a famished Esau traded his birthright for a bowl of lentils. He chose to become a hunter, the job of a warrior; an adrenaline junkie, not a leader. He wept bitterly when he discovered his blessing had been taken. Immediately, bitterness became hatred and hatred plotted murder. His father, whom he pleased by hunting and preparing delicious game for, became part of his ring of retribution in Genesis 28:8. "And Esau seeing that the daughters of Canaan pleased not Isaac his father; Then went Esau unto Ishmael, and took unto the wives which he had Mahalath the daughter of Ishmael Abraham's son, the sister of Begajoth, to be his wife."

Esau's motives were always self-serving, self-centered, and selfish. Everything he did was for personal fulfillment and gain. Yet, if you just skim the story on the surface, it seems like poor Esau's just getting the short lot out of life. But it isn't so.

Jacob, on the other hand, appears to be this great trickster, a plotter, a thief. Really, he is being obedient. I know, it's difficult to swallow, but if you study the scriptures, he stays as a herdsman learning his people and how to manage them. His mother tells him to dress in furs and feed his father for the blessing, even taking the curse upon herself and he obeys. In Genesis 28:7, after Isaac tells him not to take a wife from among the daughters of Canaan, but to go back to Uncle Laban's house, "And that Jacob obeyed his father and his mother," once again.

In verse 12, God appears to Jacob in a dream, confirming the blessing of Isaac. Why? My guess is Jacob had to have felt like he'd stolen what wasn't his.

But he hadn't. Back in Genesis 25:23, Rebecca is told two nations and two people were in her womb. One would be greater than the other and the elder should serve the younger.

So what does this all mean?

To create characters that emulate real life, you must study real life. In the story of Jacob and Esau, depending upon where you jump in, you can side with either brother, you can side with either parent, but you will always come back to the fact that God's plans are sovereign, in the same way that your plans, as your story god, out-trump your character's "plans" every time.

When writing, your characters must display human emotions of confusion, self-doubt, shame, and heartache. Or aloofness, bitterness, envy, and malice. These dynamics make great characters. We can feel their emotions as we imagine ourselves in their shoes or remember a time when we were. And a great way to accomplish this is by making things not what they appear to be.

Have you created characters the reader can empathize with regardless of their right or wrong status? (Snape and Anakin Skywalker) Will the reader feel the inner struggle as your main character fights and-or accepts their destiny whether they believe it or not? (Ender Wiggins or Katniss Everdeen) Did you remember to bring in a character to affirm the main character's role? (Glenda to Dorothy or Timothy E. Mouse to Dumbo)

Take some time to have your characters share their inner turmoil, fears, and life questions. Show their insecurities and flaws in their decisions, dialogue, and choices. Han Solo sticks in our minds because he redeems himself by returning to fight. In the whole story, he is set up as the self-absorbed, untrustworthy, emotionally-driven "Esau" of *Star Wars*. But in the end, he makes the right choice and we love him for it.

Chapter Twenty-Four:

The Love Triangle

Ah, the power of love.

Romeo and Juliet. Edward and Bella. Shrek and Fiona.

But what happens when that third person enters the scene? When Jacob vies for Bella's heart, when Katniss feels torn between Peeta and Gale, or when Prince Charming locks Shrek up and steals his identity? Plot happens, that's what.

In Genesis 29, Jacob reaches the land of his people, of Laban his uncle, where he runs into Laban's daughter, Rachel. They go back home and after a great celebration, Laban asks him what his wages should be for working his uncle's property. Jacob was in love. Mere money wouldn't do it. Food had lost its taste. "And Jacob loved Rachel; and said, I will serve thee seven years for Rachel, thy younger daughter." (verse 18) And Laban agreed. But there was a catch: Leah.

Leah was the older sister and it was customary

that the oldest daughter be married off first. Unfortunately, she was the very less attractive older sister. "Leah was tender-eyed; but Rachel was beautiful and well favoured." (verse 17) Maybe she had the hots for Jacob. Maybe she didn't. We aren't told. What we are told is that after seven years, Rebecca and Jacob wed, but with her face covered, the darkness of the bedroom, and the flow of wine, he awoke to find he'd married Leah. Laban had switched daughters, telling a furious Jacob that they don't give the younger away before the firstborn in their country. But he could work another seven years for Rachel, if he wanted.

The love triangle is set.

I find it incredibly interesting that the great trickster is tricked, a wonderful plot thread to the greater story of Jacob's life. Remember the chapter on plotting coincidence? This is another prime example in the Bible of cause and effect or sowing and reaping, where Jacob got what he dished out and then some.

Jacob hates Leah, even though it isn't her fault, and I'm sure Rachel hates her too. They're all mad at Laban, who used his daughters for slave labor payment to gain wealth, and Jacob is stuck having to work twice as long and hard for Rachel as originally promised.

Imagine the pillow talk in that house! An unloved wife, whose womb God opens, whose desire to please her husband and gain his acceptance motivates her every decision. An adored wife who has to share her husband with her sister because of her father's trickery, whose womb has been closed by God.

The things that make this love triangle work are

those who want love can't attain it and those who attain love don't have happiness. Betrayal, lies, envy, jealousy, deception, hatred, and love mingle together as the perfect story backdrop. Sounds like a Hollywood movie.

Not all stories can pull off the love triangle. But even subtle flirting or wandering eyes can add tension to scenes by bringing in a third party. It's done well with Harry, Ron, and Hermione in the beginning of the Harry Potter series as we wonder if Harry and Hermione will hook up, and where that will leave Ron, and eventually we wonder if Ron will ever get the courage to ask Hermione out as the romance shifts. It's a major plot point in the Hunger Games, as we know Katniss's loyalty lies with Gale although her heart is tugged toward Peeta. Christina Benjamin does a great job of this love triangle in her *Geneva Project* series as several suitors vie for main character Geneva's attention. Her heart aches for Nova, but when she meets Kai, it seems that her affections may shift.

How can you wedge hurtles between your lovers by bringing in a third person? Are there scenes you can alter to provide the tension from envy and jealousy, even if just for that moment? How can outside forces make a love triangle beyond your character's control? What are they going to do about it? How far are they willing to go?

Chapter Twenty-Five:

Forcing Change

Genesis chapter 30 is filled with amazing lessons, both for life and great literature. We witness the tennis match of envy and jealousy as Rachel and Leah fight for Jacob's affections. Each become pregnant, then give Jacob their handmaids for him to impregnate, which leads to God eventually opening Rachel's womb and the birth of Joseph. But that's not this chapter's focus. The secondary or B-story of the magic rod is an amazing example of forcing change in the plot, something every great author must master.

After the birth of many children, who eventually became the heads of the twelve tribes of Israel, Jacob has had enough and is ready to build a home of his own. He asks Uncle Laban for permission to leave and Laban says, "I pray thee, if I have found favour in thine eyes, tarry: for I have learned by experience that the Lord hath blessed me for thy sake." (verse 27)

Can you believe the gall of this guy? He tricked Jacob into fourteen years of indentured servitude, then eleven children later—which constitutes another large chunk of time—Laban is telling Jacob that although he is due for his own home, he wants to continue to use him to get wealthier.

Truthfully, the story has become stale. A war of the wombs ensues, trapping Jacob and his loins in the middle. He's without land to call his own and his growing family needs space. They've outgrown the guest house, the outhouse, and the farmhouse. The story could continue in this manner, but it's boring. It's time for Jacob to force change in his life and push the story along.

As a writer, you must pay attention to places in your novel where the action has slowed or halted, where too much dialogue transpires for too long, or where you have spent too much time in the same location or scene. Even readers can get cabin fever. Only they can set your book down and jump into another story leaving you and your characters agonizing through the narrative alone. Look for places in your story where you feel your mind start to wander. You know if it's not capturing your attention it won't hold your audience. Has the dialogue become redundant? Have we been through this scene already? Do we need a new setting?

In Genesis 30:29, after Laban asks Jacob what he wants for his wages, and Jacob says, "Now you ask? After I've worked for free all these years and multiplied your worth and made your rich?" Jacob had nothing but his family, while Laban sat pretty on Jacob's time. His solution? Jacob must force change.

Jacob tells Laban he would pass through the flock and remove all the speckled and spotted goats and cattle, and all the brown sheep. Basically, the rejects, the damaged, and the class B animals that wouldn't pass the "Aram Department of Agriculture" inspection. Laban agreed.

Here's where the great trickster rises once again with his magic rod to force change. "And Jacob took him rods of green poplar, and of the hazel and chestnut tree; and piled white stripes in them, and made the white appear which was in the rods." (verse 37) He separated his flock from Laban's. But when Laban's strongest cattle came to the watering hole to conceive, Jacob set the rods before them. "And the flocks conceived before the rods, and brought forth cattle ringstraked, speckled, and spotted." (verse 39) When the weak animals approached, Jacob withdrew the rods and the offspring came forth looking perfectly normal. Jacob repeated this with the sheep, the goats, and the cattle, thus building a strong, yet ugly, flock for himself and leaving behind the weaker, but beautiful, animals for Laban.

Through a magic rod, Jacob altered the physical make-up of the flocks in his favor, increasing his net value exceedingly. He forced change in his home life and moved out of Laban Land. By forcing change in the flock's appearance, he received fair wages for the decades of free labor, only Laban couldn't tell because the remaining flock looked perfect. It was a risk, yes, leaving with nothing, but the hero found a way and made things happen.

How can you force change in your story? How do you even know where to do it? What clever ways can your hero manufacture whatever they need to alter their current path? What stories can you study to learn different ways of accomplishing this?

If your story feels stale, usually after the halfway point—the muddle in the middle—it may be because you just kept going down your current story path instead of forcing a plot twist a few scenes back. Pick the spot where you feel the story lags and force a change: a death, a natural disaster, a major trickery, a needed escape. See where this change takes you and then compare it to your first version. I'm certain you won't be disappointed with the new draft, even if it doesn't look as perfect as the boring one. You'll find tension and excitement have once again returned to your plot, and you'll be back in business.

Chapter Twenty-Six:

Motivation and Lies

Building believable characters means giving them depth and emotion. Like in real life, our characters must have driving, motivating emotions that define their life choices. Sometimes, those motivations can be based in lies—the best ones often are. The lies spoken over children shape who they become in their adult lives. "You'll never amount to anything," is a lie that if swallowed will come to pass; yet if rejected, it can become the motivation that leads to success. Sometimes, the lies exist because we plant the seeds ourselves. Our perception twists the truth and that altered reality becomes our new reality, one by which we are motivated to change or destined to fall a victim to. These are qualities of humanity, which *must* be incorporated into your story world if you are ever to create characters your reader can relate to.

Genesis 31 introduces the motivation and lies of Jacob, Laban, and Rachel. Right away in verses 1 & 2,

Jacob hears Laban's sons saying, "Jacob hath taken away all that was our fathers; and of that which was our fathers hath he gotten all this glory."

Is that true? It sounds like a skewed perceptive to me. Jacob built all that Laban had, and he left with his family and the Class B "Aram Department of Agriculture" rejected animals that he created from his magic rod. But Laban bought the lie.

So Jacob sends his people away and begins to explain himself to his wives. Why? Defending against the lie he doesn't believe? Justifying his actions to convince himself it really is a lie? Pay attention to his reactions, for they are very human and should be incorporated into writing great characters. Jacob wants to make sure Laban's daughters—his wives—are on his side. He needs to know that they won't buy the lie. So in verses 4-13, he pleads his case, painting Laban as the villain and himself as the victim. "And ye know that with all my power I have served your father. And your father has deceived me and changed my wages ten times;" (verse 6-7) Jacob only did what he did because it was owed to him. He deserved it. He had earned it. He was entitled. Couldn't his wives understand?

Oh, and they did!

But they read between the lines of Jacob's story. See, Jacob went on and on how he had worked for twenty-five years and had his wages changed all those times, in reference to Rebecca and Leah. They had been bought. They belonged to him. That's what they heard, and the sisters bought the lie that they had been sold as slaves by their own father. "And Rachel and Leah answered and said unto him, Is there yet any portion of inheritance for us in our father's house? Are we not counted of him strangers? for he hath sold us, and hath quite devoured also our money." (verse 15)

Ouch! They all bought into a lie which motivated them into action: Jacob believed he was justified and it motivated him to trick Laban and leave in the middle of the night with all his possessions. He also believed Laban's countenance had fallen on account of Laban's son's lies that Jacob, through Laban, believed too. Fear also motivated him to leave—coincidentally, I believe fear is what kept him there working for free all those years. His response to his situation was all that changed. Rebecca and Leah believed that Jacob was justified in his thievery, as those riches technically belonged to them as the bride's dowry. But Rebecca took it further. Perhaps her hurt ran deeper. She bought the lie that she had been sold like a slave and I think this reality surprised her. See, Leah had always been second best. She easily swallowed the lie and moved past it; accepted it. Rebecca, on the other hand, was her father's beloved. Daddy's little girl. A princess. ("Funny, she doesn't look Druish.") She felt betrayed and wanted retribution. So, she attacked what she knew to be Daddy's prized possessions: his gods. The statues he worshipped. You hurt me, I hurt you. Motivation.

A week out, Laban catches up to them. He accuses Jacob of all his wrongs and demands a search of the camp to retrieve his stolen statues. When they are not found (because they are strapped beneath Rebecca who claims to be on her period and unable to stand), Jacob goes ballistic! He goes off on Laban, reminding him of everything he has done over the past twenty years.

What's interesting here is that this time, the lie is so ingrained that Jacob speaks it as if it's truth. He is no longer justifying, as he had to his wives, but rather proclaiming in rage this injustice that has befallen him. In the end, Laban and Jacob place stones in a pile to represent a barrier wall between them as a covenant that neither will ever cross in malice. Motivation. Truly, the motivation and lies in this chapter cause them to all be right in their own way, just like in real life. There is a whole lot of gray between black and white.

I am reminded of my two favorite characters in literature: Ender Wiggins and Katniss Everdeen. Ender is so afraid of the lie that he will become a ruthless killer just like his brother that he works tirelessly to become nothing like him. Only, when push comes to shove, he does what is necessary to survive, and his ultimate fears are realized. He has become the killer he desperately tried to avoid. In reality, he just began to see life through the filter of his self-induced lie. Everything he does is motivated through this lens. Likewise, Katniss Everdeen believes the lie that she has one up on the Capitol; sneaking in the woods to hunt in District 12, selling meat in the Hob black market, eating the berries with Peeta. She soon learns in *Catching Fire* that her lies are mere illusions and she controls nothing. Only when she is able to accept this truth is she ready to see the world for what it really is. Who else comes to mind? Neo from *The Matrix*. Mr. Hillyer from *The Time Machine*. Wolverine from *X-Men*.

Have you built in lies to each of your characters

personalities? How do these lies motivate them? Do you show the lie grow from conception to justification to acceptance as truth? What ways can you have your characters see life through the lens of their lies?

Think of some of the lies in your own life and the lives of others that have been accepted as truth. How does that affect your relationships? Pay attention to how these lies motivate people into either stagnant acceptance or aggressive resistance. Use it in your novel.

Chapter Twenty-Seven:

Seeing God

In your story world, you play the role of God. You are the unseen narrator in third person voice and the thoughts, actions, and dialogue in first person voice. You are every character in your story in one way or another. As the main character and sidekicks, you imagine how you would respond in the given situation. What would your friends do or say? As the antagonist, you may question, "What wouldn't I do in this predicament? How wouldn't I react or reply?" Background characters may be a reflection of those people around you like extras in a movie or television show. They are there to bring a deeper level or realism to your scene and nothing more.

In this way of thinking, it is appropriate to say that you are both the characters and the story god at the same time. But what happens when your characters stop listening? What do you do when you uncover something in your character that reveals a deep flaw within yourself? You can no longer control them. You no longer can predict their words or actions. It's almost as if the character has become the story god, dictating events while you have become a whimsical character lost in the white space of your page. So what do you do? You wrestle for your power back.

Near the end of Genesis 32, Jacob is left alone in the wilderness. His brother, Esau, is approaching with his men. Jacob has sent gifts of animals; "Two hundred she goats, and twenty he goats, two hundred ewes, and twenty rams, thirty milch camels with their colts, forty kine, and ten bulls, twenty she asses, and ten foals." (verses 14-15) Quite a massive present. Think maybe Jacob felt a little bit guilty? Afraid for his life, perhaps?

Next, Jacob split up the rest of his possessions into groups creating space between each drove, should some harm be headed their way, leaving his family for the last group. But this wasn't a vacation for Jacob. "And Jacob was left alone; and there wrested a man with him until the breaking of day." (verse 24) He wrestled this person all night long, kind of like you with your misbehaving characters.

And what did this person do at daybreak? "And when he saw that he (Jacob) prevailed not against him, he touched the hollow of his thigh; and the hollow of Jacob's thigh was out of joint as he wrestled with him." (verse 25) He gave him a permanent limp. He changed Jacob's physical makeup which altered his future, in order to gain the upper hand. He changed the projection of his story. "And he said, Let me go, for the day breaketh. And he (Jacob) said, I will not let thee go, except thou bless me." (verse 26)

Why is any of this relevant? Because Jacob is wrestling with God. "And Jacob called the name of the place Peniel: for I have seen God face to face, and my life is preserved." (verse 30) Jacob faces God. God forces change. God wins.

In your story world, you will occasionally face a character who needs wrestling, and most often it's your own shortcoming you are facing within the characters you've created. Our characters reflect us. When they make weak choices, they are our weak choices. When they cower, it's because we cower. When they jump in without thinking, they are doing what we would do.

Our characters draw out our own imperfections, much like our children do, and unless we wrestle them by letting them see "god" our novels will never reach the potential and depth they deserve. What ways can you wrestle with your characters? Are there permanent inflictions, either physical or emotional, that you can force on your character to get them in line? How do you resolve your own issues within the pages of your book? Writing can be a cathartic experience for not just the reader, but for you as the writer. It can be a place to share or express fears, opinions, and issues that you may not have the courage to say out loud in the real world. Just be certain that if you give your character a bold voice or force them to relive your painful experiences that you are ready to face the consequences in the real world.

Chapter Twenty-Eight:

The Storm Before the Calm

Conflict and drama are great for fiction, but as in real life, if there is no restoration you lose all hope. Conflicts need to be resolved, whether it be the main story problem or the minor ones along the way. These moments drive the story and keep the reader hanging on each page. These moments allow characters to develop and grow. These moments define your story.

In Genesis 33, the big moment arrives. After a lifetime of worries and fear, and after presents have been delivered, Jacob finally faces Esau for the first time since he left home after tricking him and stealing his blessing. "And Jacob lifted up his eyes, and looked, and, behold, Esau came, and with four hundred men." (verse 2)

What we don't read about is how Jacob must have been feeling. What thoughts were running through his head? What physiological responses was his body going through? Was he literally trembling?

114

The inferred tension in this scene is tremendous. And it should be. It is the final action before the climax.

Think of it as the storm before the calm.

The level of emotions vying for the spotlight during this moment could be unbearable if you didn't face the conflict and push through. The scene in *The Hunger Games* where Peeta and Katniss head toward the cornucopia and hear the growl of the genetically altered creatures is one of those moments. Peeta asks what the sound is and Katniss answers, "The finale." It's the storm on the horizon and its coming fast.

In *Back to the Future*, one of my favorites, the final moments before Doc sends Marty back are excruciating. The Doc won't listen to his future fate, the branch unplugs the cord, the car won't start, the plug separates a second time, the lighting strikes, and BAM! It all works out. Everything goes calm. The lightning stops, the winds cease, the DeLorean is gone. The storm before the calm.

In Genesis 33:8, Jacob literally lays at Esau's feet.

The storm.

Will Esau chop off his bowed head? Will he rehash the past? Will he belittle and verbally abuse his kid brother? Esau asks, "What meanest thou by all this drove which I met?"

The first thing he says is, "Dude, what's up with the ridiculous caravan of gifts?"

Jacob must be totally thrown off because he answers, "These are to find grace in the sight of my lord." Duh! Here they go back and forth about to take, or not to take the drove, ending with a reconciliation, a no hard feelings—no grudge held approach from Eau and a humble heart of servitude from Jacob.

The calm.

These moments must occur in your story, and not just as the climactic moment. The climax is essential, but building in smaller storms that lead to calm moments will keep your reader swinging between fear and hope. It will build tension and provide relief as the story swells toward that final storm.

Have you built up your story arc to the steepest angle possible before reaching the climax? In what ways can you amp up the storm before the calm? Can you add in minor plot points that bring about tension that is resolved in restoration?

Remember, too much tension is just as bad as not enough if you don't bring it to a head. Hope drives the stories in the Bible, in our lives, and should also drive the story you're writing. Showing your characters facing many storms, and then providing both them and the reader a break in that calm period will allow everyone to breath and gear up for what's to come. A brilliant author who utilizes this is James Dashner in the *Maze Runner* series. I literally felt sorry for the characters as they faced trial after trial, storm after storm, making those calm moments that much sweeter and necessary. The storms are what make great fiction, but without the calms that follow, the reader would never have the chance to reflect on life lessons with the characters and growth wouldn't be possible.

Chapter Twenty-Nine:

Tell, Don't Show

I know, I know. Your jaw just dropped. What kind of a writing book is this? What writer instructs others to break the most basic of all cardinal rules, Show, Don't Tell? This one, right here. Let me show you why.

After Jacob and Esau reconcile, "Jacob journeyed to Shalam a city of Shechem; which is in the land of Caanan." (verse 18) In Genesis 34, "Dinah the daughter of Leah, which she bare unto Jacob, went out to see the daughters of the land." (verse 1) While out, she is taken by Shechem, son of Hamor who lay with and defile her. Pretty hard core. Now, while the story doesn't specify, it sounds like this wasn't consensual to say the least, and both her daddy and brothers are seeing red.

Shechem's father, Hamor, steps in, presenting Jacob with a deal, requesting he give Dinah's hand to Shechem in marriage, being so bold as to suggest to Jacob, "Give your daughters unto us and take our daughters unto you." (verse 9)

So what does any of this have to do with Show, Don't Tell? "And the sons of Jacob answered Shechem and Hamor his father deceitfully." (verse 13) Woah. Did they know this? The answer is most assuredly "no, they did not," because they agreed to the unorthodox demand of Jacob's sons, which I'll go into in a minute. In verse 13, the reader is given a piece of information that is unbeknownst to all of the characters in the scene. The narrator has spoken directly to the audience giving them a glimpse into how this story might unfold.

Tell, Don't Show.

Why does the work? Think of the many stories that use this tool successfully. We know Anakin Skywalker is flirting with the Dark Side before he slays younglings and pledges allegiance to Count Dooku. We know the Titanic will sink, even as we witness Rose and Jack falling in forbidden love. And we know Ariel is the real woman that the prince fell in love with and that Ursula has stolen her voice in order to pose as her. How then do we stay interested and engaged as readers? The characters.

We have all felt heartache, betrayal, and hope. We can relate to the confusion and frustration of the characters as they navigate through the story toward events that we, the reader, already know to be inevitable. It's our emotional rollercoaster, the turmoil of others that we are able to experience for the briefest moment before we are out of the book and back to our normal lives.

The point is to know when to tell the audience a detail in advance and when to withhold and show.

Ironically, stories told in the first person voice can know things other characters don't know, which are immediately revealed to the reader through eye witness accounts, inner dialogue, and personal discovery. But the character cannot know things they do not see or hear, which means neither can the reader.

Why choose the reveal? Tension.

In Genesis 34, the sons of Jacob are grieved and wroth over Dinah's defilement. They decide to go in like a Trojan horse by agreeing to Hamor's proposition only under one condition. "Only herein will the men consent unto us for to dwell with us, to be one people, if every male among us be circumcised, as they are circumcised." (verse 22) And Hamor agrees. Tension heightens.

As a reader, you may begin to become angry, so much so that you could stop reading. What is going on? How have they consented so easily? A wrong has been done and a villain has been rewarded. It's completely unfair, you holler. How could they? But then, you remember that one little word that changes everything: And the sons of Jacob answered Shechem and Hamor his father *deceitfully*." Deceitfully. Ah, yes. There is more to this story than what we are shown. Something is happening behind the scenes, so we continue to read, filled with hope (and not anger).

"...and every male was circumcised, all that went out of the gate of his city." (verse 24)

Well, the story looks like they aren't going to avenge Dinah's disgrace. No, no...wait. Deceitfully. Okay, keep reading. "And it came to pass on the third day, when they were sore, that two of the sons of Jacob. Simeon and Levi, Dinah's brethren, took each man his sword, and came upon the city boldly, and slew all males. And they slew Hamor and Shechem his son with the edge of the sword, and took Dinah out of Shechem's house and went out." (verse 25-26)

Oh, now we feel justified. Now we feel satisfaction as readers. We followed the story to completion, even though we worried there for awhile that things wouldn't work how we'd hoped. Thankfully, we were told that little hint about the deceitfulness of the sons of Jacob or the tension would have outweighed our curiosity as a reader, and we never would have made it to the end.

Do you have a place in your story where the reader may feel frustrated or find themselves mad at the choices you've made because you're not sharing enough or a crucial component? Could it be you have withheld information to make the climax a surprise? If they never finish your book, who is going to be surprised? You as the author, that's who. How can you deliver this information through a Tell, Don't Show, in a way that is both believable and necessary to your characters and plot?

It's great to string your reader along for a small bit of time or to not share details in order to reveal something later. But if it brings frustration rather than nervousness or anger rather than hope, you will only give the wrong type of tension to your audience. And people won't sustain that feeling for a whole novel.

Chapter Thirty:

Death and Taxes

Two things in life are certain, they say: death and taxes.

In Genesis 35, we come across one of those. After some time, God instructs Jacob to pick up and "go to Bethel, and dwell there: and make there an alter." (verse 1) He sends him back to where he fled from Esau. I believe this is more than a geographical cure, because in verse 2, Jacob tells his household, "Put away the strange gods that are among you, and be clean, and change your garments."

It seems that Jacob read between the lines here and saw that God wanted to bring Jacob and his people back to a place of dependency upon him. They had become too ingrained with the culture around them, too comfortable to need God. Bringing Jacob back to the place of desperation where, out of fear for his life, he clung to God, would remind them of God's great promises and the fact that they were called out as a people.

In fact, in verses 9-12, God visits with Jacob not only reminding him of the promises he had made to his father and grandfather, which would be fulfilled through him, but He also again changes his name form Jacob (Trickster) to Israel (Strives with God). Perhaps after all this time, Jacob has grown into his name. Maybe it finally fits. He has been a man driven by emotion all his life, by pleasure and fleshly lusts, balanced between the meticulous planning of a trickster. Could it be that Jacob finally got it?

Why now? Because God knew what was coming.

In verse 16, they caravanned to Ephrath where Rachel, Jacob's beloved, experienced hard labor. The midwife assured her that her son would live, but "and it came to pass, as her soul was departing (for she died) that she called his name Ben-oni: but his father called him Benjamin." Rachel died in childbirth.

Imagine Jacob's heartbreak. Imagine Leah's guilty relief and sorrow. God knew this moment was coming. Death and taxes. He knew Jacob was not prepared for it. I think that's why Jacob was brought back to the same spot where he wrestled God fact to face; to the same place where God changed his name to Israel. It seems Jacob's life had swerved from God's divine path and he needed to be rerouted. Same place, different perspective.

This time prepared him for Rachel's death and the birth of his second son from the wife he truly loved. In the Hebrew, Rachel named the child "son of sorrow and grief" (Ben-oni), but Jacob changed his name to "child of joy and comfort and blessing":

Benjamin.

Death is a part of life. Sometimes, our characters lose loved ones. Other times, our main characters must die. In each case, it is our job as story god to prepare the story for the tragedy in advance.

In *Star Wars Revenge of the Sith*, Padme dies in childbirth while giving birth to Luke and Leah (sound familiar???). We are heartbroken, even though we are warned this travesty would come through Anakin's visions and dreams. Chancellor Palpatine promises him the power to save his loved ones from death, if he sides with the Dark Side. And the very thing Anakin tries to prevent (his inability to save Padme like he couldn't save his mother) becomes the very thing that brings on Padme's death and Anakin's ultimate decision to join the Dark Side of the Force.

In *The Hunger Games*, Rue's death is inevitable. She reminds Katniss of Primrose, she is young and helpless, and they have formed an alliance. We know Katniss will survive the games (or at least we hope) since she's the main character. We also know that Rue won't. Funny how the story deals with both inevitables at once: death of the tributes in the game as taxes.

Sometimes, the main character has to go. We know from the beginning that Harry and Voldemort from the Harry Potter series will ultimately face off in a final battle to the death. Our little Harry has a chance. Then, we learn that while one lives, the other must die. When we discover the deep-rooted connection they share, we realize with horror that Harry will die. And when it happens, we feel helpless and empty inside, as if we've just lost a best friend, because in reality, we have.

As your story god, you will have to make those hard decision to take life from your story world. The trick is making it a result of your plot and not plotting it as a means to an end. Does this person's death strengthen the main character's need to drive them toward resolving their inner conflict? Does removing this character from the story force others to rise to the challenge? Is there a strong enough emotional connection established between the reader and the character, as well as the protagonist and the character for it to matter?

Many stories deal with death, and it makes sense, since it's one of two things in life the we must all face. Building a death scene into your story can be a powerful tool if executed properly (no pun intended). Showing "life must go on" builds character in your characters and builds a bridge between your story world and the world of your reader.

Chapter Thirty-One:

Symbolism and Dreams

I was led to write this book while studying the story of Joseph. As I read through the story, I noticed for the first time that in both instances when Joseph was thrown into a pit, he had been stripped of his robes first, which represented his status in life. How had I missed that before? I realized God used literary devices in story. Foreshadow. Symbolism. The Power of 3s. The list goes on. It was at this moment when the idea struck me to study the Bible from an author's perspective. This book is my attempt, and this chapter introduces the story of Joseph.

Genesis 37 begins when Joseph is seventeen. He is with his brothers tending the animals, but returns home to tell on them. He is the firstborn of Israel (Jacob) and his beloved Rachel, and he favors him big time. "Now Israel loved Joseph more than all his children, because he was the son of his old age: and he made him a coat of many colors." (verse 3) This coat symbolizes his father's love for him. It symbolizes his status as his father's favorite. Imagine working with animals all day long (ever been to a petting zoo or farm?) with the smells and the dirt the job brings with it. Now, picture your baby brother strolling out wearing his Armani with stitching made from white gold. He's not working; he's spying, for dear old dad. And while you slave away to pay the bills, baby brother gets the spoil.

But it gets worse.

In verse 2, he brings unto his father the evil report of his brothers in the field. This implies he is a good judge of character and that he is walking with the Lord, in my mind. Then, in verses 5-9, Joseph begins to dream. "And he said unto them, Hear, I pray you, this dream which I have dreamed: For behold, we were binding sheaves in the field, and, lo, my sheaf arose, and also stood upright; and, behold, your sheaves stood round about, and made obeisance to my sheaf." (verse 6-7)

Nanny, nanny, boo-boo!

Joseph is just digging the knife deeper. But what does this reveal about the nature of his character? Does he share this dream to flaunt his stuff? It doesn't seem that way, more oblivion than anything else. And the fact that he openly shares this dream with his brothers, who openly hate him, as a matter of truth, tells me the strength of his convictions and that he fears God above all else.

Utilizing dreams is one of my favorite tools as an author. In dreams, you can show foreshadowing and reveal traits unseen by the character through their subconscious that builds the plot. Dreams can add layers and dimensions through symbolism and imagery in a way that no other writing device can. And the truth is revealed to the characters in different ways, viewed through their own lens of lies, misconceptions, and judgments.

"And he dreamt yet another dream, and told it to his brethren and said, Behold, I have dreamed a dream more; and, behold, the sun and the moon and the eleven stars made obeisance to me." (verse 9)

Now, daddy Israel steps in: "Shall I and thy mother and thy brethren indeed come to bow down ourselves to thee to the earth?" (verse 10)

I love the way the second dream expands on the first one. It's the same dream in essence, but now it includes Joseph's parents too, which is the exact order of events to come. These symbolic dreams come to pass in Genesis chapter 42 and are a fabulous example of foreshadowing through symbolism.

As you work through your manuscript, are there any places you can add symbolic dreams to foreshadow the story's climax? Can you take something literal and make it vaguer through picture meaning or definitions? Have you considered incorporating a dream dictionary to take the dreams you have already built into your story and give them more cryptic meaning?

As I've already mentioned, this story of Joseph birthed the idea for this book. It is filled with literary tools, which I will continue to explore for a good portion of the rest of this guide.

Chapter Thirty-Two:

Inferring Behind the Scenes

Joseph is a fabulous example of a great hero. His entire journey, from spoiled son to ruler of Egypt, is one that should be studied in depth by every author. In Genesis 37:12, he begins his hero's quest as his father sends him out to check on his brothers. This is after Joseph has shared his dreams of superiority over his entire family, after his brothers' envy has taken a stronghold on them and grown into hatred. "And when they saw him afar off, even before he came near unto them, they conspired against him to slay him." (verse 18)

This is so important; sibling rivalry built over many years. Wounds grew and deepened. New lies took root. The brothers worked together in the field all day long while Joseph stayed home as Daddy's perfect son, who was too good to get his hands dirty (or his coat of many colors, for that matter). Imagine how they gossiped and plotted against Joseph. Family has a tendency to talk about family very cruelly behind one another's backs. Their hatred swelled until that one day when Joseph appeared and they decided to act and kill him. "And they said one to another, Behold, this dreamer cometh." (verse 19)

The takeaway here is that all of this occurred off the pages. We infer this growth of animosity and the conversations in the field that provided the fuel. We imagine what they felt and side in sympathy. But none of this is found in the text; yet as a reader, we still figure it out. We still get it. We don't have to be told everything.

Building frustration and motivation into your plot through inference will allow you to suddenly have a group of characters plotting murder without the reader blinking an eye. Too often plot points occur that feel convenient or surprising because they don't make sense, not because they can't. In other words, all the author needs to do is establish a few moments to frame what's happening behind the scenes and the reader can fill in the rest through inference filtered by their own experiences.

So Joseph nears, and we read in verse 20, "Come now therefore, and let us slay him, and cast him into some pit, and we will say, Some evil beast hath devoured him: and we shall see what will become of his dreams."

They are extremely jaded over those dreams, aren't they? So they grab Joseph, strip him of his coat—the representation of his status in his father's family—and throw him into the pit. Then, they have lunch, deciding instead to make some money off their brother rather than just killing him. He is, after all, their flesh and blood. "Come, and let us sell him to the

Ishmaelites, and let not our hands be upon him; for he is our brother and our flesh. And his (Judah's) brethren were content." (verse 27)

So now, they lift Joseph from the pit and sell him. I can't imagine this was a simple transaction. I doubt Joseph sat quietly. I don't know because it isn't in the text, but I can use what I read and what I know to fill in the story framework. He either kicked, writhed, and screamed, or his brothers beat him inches from death to stay quiet. Regardless, Joseph is now on his way to Egypt. The hero's quest has begun.

His brothers kill goats and smear the blood on the torn up coat to make Jacob believe Joseph was killed by a wild animal. As mentioned previously, this is another thread in Jacob's life where the great trickster is tricked; first by waking up to find he'd married Leah, and now losing his favorite son from his beloved Rachel. It seems he bore the curse of tricking his father from Esau's blessing after all. This is the last we see of the family until the great famine many years later. In the meantime, Joseph is sold unto Potiphar in Egypt, who is second in command beneath only Pharaoh.

It's incredible how well built and perfectly timed this portion of scripture is revealed. So much remains untold, yet the reader can follow along clearly by stringing together the few concrete details provided and relying on their own inference through experience to fill in the rest.

In your story, have you given too many details? Have you provided side story that doesn't keep the story flowing naturally? Where can you remove information, relying on the intellect of the reader to fill in the blanks?

Humans share many feelings and reactions. Many are simply variations, which grow in scale as a direct result of wounds and lies. Envy becomes jealousy becomes hatred becomes vengeance becomes murder. If you give a few details of a jealous character and then later, show them plotting revenge, your reader can infer the decline in emotion. They can decide the character is suffering from envy. An anxious character can easily develop paranoia with time, and if you show them reacting out of fear and desperation, the reader can infer the rest.

Try observing characters in movies or television shows you know well. Decide which core emotion they are exhibiting, then list the varying degrees associated with it. Where are they in the spectrum? Where can they go from here? How can you show one or two details to let the reader infer the rest? Remember, the greater the spiral from normal, the steeper the climb back to emotional equilibrium and the more tension you will build into your narrative.

Chapter Thirty-Three:

Subplots

Every great plot has equally great subplots. The 'B' story, if you will. Some are even so amazing that spinoffs featuring these stories often result. Most times, they are based off profound characters such as *X-Men's* Wolverine, *Pitch Black's* Riddick, and *Star Wars's* Anakin Skywalker. In Genesis chapter 38, Joseph is out of the scene and we focus on his brother, Judah.

Judah marries a Canaanite woman and they have a couple kids who grow up and marry. "And Er, Judah's firstborn, was wicked in the sight of the Lord; and the Lord slew him." (verse 7) In this day and age, when an in-law was widowed, it became the responsibility of the deceased's siblings to impregnate the widow to carry on the namesake. Judah tells his son, Onan, to complete this task to honor his brother's memory. "And Onan knew that the seed should not be his; and it came to pass, when he went in unto his brother's wife, that he spilled it on the ground, lest that he should give seed to his brother." (verse 9)

Guess what? God slew him too. So Judah told her to stay a widow in his house and when his son, Shelah, was grown, she could marry him. In the meantime, Judah's wife died and Shelah grew, but was not betrothed to Tamar. Here's where the story gets good.

She pretends to be a harlot in a strange town where Judah has gone to work temporarily and seduces her father-in-law. He offers to pay her a goat for her services to which she requests proof of his word in the form of a pledge. "And he said, What pledge shall I give thee? And she said, Thy signet and thy bracelets, and thy staff that is in thy hand. And he gave it her, and came in unto her, and she conceived by him." (verse 18)

Basically, she had his DNA – blood and hair samples of that day and age – his signet to undeniably mark him as the father. Later, when she shows the pregnancy, she is accused of playing the harlot and brought before Judah for punishment. She shows him the pledged items and proclaims that the man who owns them is the father. With head between his legs, Judah admits his unrighteousness.

Why this side story? Genesis 37 is about Joseph thrown in the pit, then sold into slavery. Genesis 39 picks right back up again with Joseph in Egypt. Perhaps, it is because of all the brothers, the only two mentioned by name are Judah and Reuben. In Genesis 37:26-27, Judah saves Joseph's life: "What profit is it if we slay our brother, and conceal his blood? Come, and let us sell him to Ishmaelites, and let not our hand be upon him; for he is our brother and our flesh." Most likely, this apparent subplot occurs to show the birth of Teran's twins who are in the direct lineage of Judah leading to the birth of Jesus, which is the main plot line of the entire Bible.

In your stories, it is crucial to weave in subplots that affect your secondary character's lives and give them the motivation they need to organically product their decisions. If they have no believable lives of their own, they will come across as fixtures whose only purpose is to assist or interfere with the main character's plight.

Who are your book's primary secondary characters? What motivates them? Do they have a subplot that **needs** (keyword: *needs*) to be shared in order to reveal something about the character that the reader *must* know in order to move the story forward?

There's a great difference between back-story and subplot. While sometimes they are one in the same, the back-story is usually an enhancement to the literary experience while the subplot is integral. Who knows, if done correctly, you could create a subplot that is so phenomenal that it can carry its own storyline.

Chapter Thirty-Four:

Ups & Downs

In a perfect world, we find safety in the belief that if we follow the rules, good things will happen. We eat right, exercise, pay our taxes, and follow the golden rule expecting life to be smooth and the "Universe" to reward us for our good deeds. In the same way, we expect the bad guys to pay for their wrongs, for justice to prevail, for the consequence to fit the crime. But life doesn't always work that way. Non-smokers get lung cancer. Serial killers don't get caught. Life just isn't fair.

When the characters in your book are facing unfair consequences, the reader feels enraged. They will demand justice. The story universe is imbalanced and must be fixed. Already, Joseph is the victim of his brothers' jealousy. They sell him into slavery. Now, we are reunited with Joseph in Genesis 39. "And Joseph was brought down to Egypt; and Potiphar, an officer of Pharaoh, captain of the guard, an Egyptian, brought him of the hands of the Ishmaelites, which had brought him down tither."

Joseph is God's main man, so everything Joseph does is blessed. He is prosperous and his master notices. "And Joseph found grace in his sight, and he served him: and he made him overseer over his house, and all that he had put into his hands." (verse 4)

We feel justified that Joseph is getting some good news after his bad situation with his brothers' deceit. But bad things happen to good people. Potiphar's wife takes notice of the handsome Hebrew her husband hired. She tells him to lie with her. But our pure, wholesome, God-fearing Joseph refuses saying, "Your husband has entrusted me with everything he has. Why would I ever do something so stupid?" Or in verse 9, "...how then can I do this great wickedness, and sin against God?" He is a Boy Scout, isn't he? However, she persists for many days, until one particular day when they are alone: "She caught him by his garment, saying, Lie with me: and he left his garment in her hand, and fled, and got him out." (verse 12)

Joseph literally leaves his clothes behind to get away from her, thinking he is doing what's righteous. What does she do? Rape whistle. She calls the guards, accusing Joseph of attempting to rape her and holds his garments in her hand as proof.

Of course, we know no one will believe this outrageous claim. After all, Joseph is a saint. He has already been wrongfully sold to Potiphar. Surely, he won't face further repercussions from this lie. "And Joseph's master took him, and put him into prison, a place where the king's prisoners were bound: and he was there in the prison." (verse 20)

Can this be true? How? That woman lied, yet her words put Joseph into prison! As a reader, we are committed to this journey, expecting to witness Joseph's final redemption because it's the right thing. Good guys always win, don't they?

Employing this technique, with your character rising and falling as a result to the decisions of others, will build a tremendous amount of genuine sympathy from the reader. We have all been betrayed and wrongfully accused, so we can easily relate to this feeling and to our expectations of eventual retribution. The truth will be revealed!

Can you supply a scene in your story where your hero is wrongfully accused and punished for no reason? How does he react? Does she patiently wait for the truth to be uncovered or go down kicking and screaming?

In some novels, this is the basis of the entire plot. A wrongfully accused hero spends his journey proving his innocence. Weave in failures and compound the accusation. Plant evidence that points fingers at your heroine. Just remember that even when the world looks bleak, and darkness reigns, the reader can always find hope...in the next chapter.

Chapter Thirty-Five:

New Characters in the Middle

Each story has a basic beginning, middle, and end; an Act I, Act II, and Act III. In Joseph's story, his beginning would be his time at home up until he is sold into slavery by his brothers (his point of no return). His end would be the following few chapters in Genesis where he is in charge of the entire country of Egypt, beneath only Pharaoh, and faces his brother for the first time (his story climax). Joseph's middle then, is here, in Genesis chapter 10.

The middle section of the story is the place of the character's lowest points. They are beat up and tired (if you're a good author) facing a place where they are alone and abandoned, probably ready to throw in the towel and give up. This is where we find Joseph. He is in the king's prison wrongfully accused (again) and thrown underground (again). His saving grace and our hope as a reader comes from Genesis 39:23: "The keeper of the prison looked not to any thing that was under his hand; because the Lord was with him (Joseph), and that which he did, the Lord made it to prosper."

Honestly, I don't think we could have handled anymore as a reader if Joseph didn't catch these breaks of favor in the sight of his captors.

In chapter 40, two new characters enter the scene and put a new spin on the story we hadn't seen coming. The baker and butler of the king had offended him, and been imprisoned alongside Joseph. And they both had dreams in the same night, which they could not interpret. "And Joseph said unto them, Do not interpretations belong to God? Tell me them, I pray you." (verse 8)

The butler shares his dream: three branches were budding grapes that he pressed into the king's cup as wine. Joseph explains the meaning; "Yet within three days shall Pharaoh lift up thine head, and restore thee unto thy place." (verse 13) Taking the opportunity, Joseph asks the butler to remember him when he is restored, "For indeed I was stolen away out of the land of the Hebrews: and here also have I done nothing that they should put me into the dungeon." (verse 15)

Seeing the favorable interpretation, the baker shares his dream, to which Joseph tells him, "Yet within three days shall Pharaoh lift up thy head from off thee, and shall hang thee on a tree; and the birds shall eat thy flesh from off thee." (verse 19)

Ouch!

So day three comes and goes, and Joseph's

interpretations come to pass. But the butler forgets all about Joseph.

So what was the point? Why introduce these characters only to have them whisked away, taking our hope for Joseph's freedom with them? Remember, we are in the middle of Joseph's story building toward the end and the climax. These characters will return, well the butler will at least, and we will understand why they were introduced in Genesis 40.

What can we learn as writers from this chapter? Characters have purpose. They aren't haphazardly introduced for no reason, nor are they all introduced in the first chapter. Plot twists occur by the pressure these new characters place on our hero. In *Ender's Game*, Petra Arkanian is introduced in the middle of the story and she impacts Ender's next moves, enabling him to enter the climax; giving him the experience and friendship he needs to succeed.

Although we meet Rue early in the *Hunger Games* during the "fun and games" section, it is the friendship she provides and ally she becomes for Katniss that matters. Rue gives Katniss the determination she needs to press on till the ending, not to mention she saves her life twice.

What new characters need to be introduced into your story to push your main character to the ending? Do you have essential information that needs to be delivered to the MC and the reader? How can you bring in the perfect new character to deliver the message?

New characters are great to keep the middle fresh, give the main character hope, and push the story toward climax. Sometimes, they are so remarkable they become staples in the series or even go on to star in stories of their own.

Chapter Thirty-Six:

Anticipating the Foreshadowed

Joseph has been through a lot of ups and downs over the past fifteen years. Sold into slavery, elevated in his master's house, unjustly accused, thrown into prison, interpreting dreams that came true, forgotten by the dreamer and left in prison; but his luck is about to change.

Two years after the cupbearer was restored to his position in Pharaoh's court, Pharaoh dreamed. His first dream was of seven fat cattle devoured by seven decimated cattle, only their appearance remained unchanged even after consuming the fatter ones. The second dream was of seven healthy ears of corn eaten by seven thin ears of corn. And he was troubled.

I love how this is the third encounter of dreams in the story of Joseph. The cool part is that as a reader, we have seen Joseph's interpretation come to pass once, which leads us to believe he knows what he's doing. After he interprets Pharaoh's dreams in this chapter, and they come true, we are sold. He definitely is a dream interpreter. This immediately takes us back to the beginning when Joseph dreamt his dreams in Genesis chapter 37. He and his brothers were binding sheaves when his sheaf stood and his brother's sheaves bowed around his. Then his second dream when the sun, moon, and eleven stars bowed to him. Now, we are true believers.

As a reader, I anticipate the foreshadowed dream events coming to pass. I have been shown the validity of Joseph's ability in the story and have developed certain expectations, which should come to pass before and during the climax. This adds tremendous tension to the story as I lobby alongside the main character rallying for my assumptions to play out. Hopefully.

Back to Genesis chapter 41...

No one can interpret Pharaoh's two dreams, and then the cupbearer remembers Joseph. He tells Pharaoh about Joseph, the dream interpreter, who predicted the cupbearer's restoration and the death of the baker. "Then Pharaoh sent and called Joseph, and they brought him hastily out of the dungeon: and he shaved himself and changed his raiment, and came in unto Pharaoh." (verse 14)

Pharaoh shares his dreams to which Joseph quickly states, "The dream of Pharaoh is one: God hath shewed Pharaoh what he is about to do." (verse 25) Joseph explains the meaning of the seven cows and seven ears of corn as seven years of plenty followed by seven years of famine. He tells Pharaoh to find someone wise to put in charge. And this is where Joseph finally receives his redemption that the reader has been waiting for. "And Pharaoh said unto Joseph, Forasmuch as God hath shewed thee all this, there is none so discreet and wise as thou art." (verse 39)

And it happens again: Joseph is restored to a position of power over the people, given a new cloak to show his ranking, and moves closer to fulfilling his purpose.

Have you clearly shown your foreshadowed events coming to pass in your story? Did you include enough supporting data through scenes earlier in the book to make the outcome believable? Is there a pattern of moments that you can go back through and weave tighter together through threads of foreshadow?

Those foreshadowed segments should be subtle, but their impact should be glaring. Think of ways in which this tool is used in stories you love. Would the event have held as much punch without the foreshadow leading to it? The role of Gollum in Frodo's quest, as foreshadowed by Gandalf, plays out when Frodo and Gollum battle over the ring on Mount Doom, even unto death. Professor Quirrel's "obsession" with Harry Potter seems fanatical, until we understand he is Lord Voldemort's vessel in *The Sorcerer's Stone*. In *Twilight*, Stephenie Myer used Bella's gift to subconsciously block out Edward from reading her mind, and as an ability to form a shield against powers once she becomes a vampire in *Breaking Dawn*. Subtle, but powerful. That's what makes a great foreshadow.

Chapter Thirty-Seven:

The Red Herring

The Red Herring is a great literary device used to force attention off the central issue and onto something else. In Genesis chapter 42, the great famine is in full swing. Every people and nation is afflicted. Starvation is widespread, though Egypt's reputation has also spread: WE HAVE FOOD.

The land of Canaan has nothing left to give, so Jacob sends his sons to Egypt to buy food. "But Benjamin, Joseph's brother, Jacob sent not with his brethren, for he said, Lest peradventure mischief befall him." (verse 4)

The brothers arrive, their packs filled with coin, and Joseph recognizes them. His dreams. His position. "And Joseph knew his brethren, but they knew him not." (verse 8) So he did what any little brother who had been sold into slavery by his brothers would do: He spoke roughly and accused them of being spies.

"And he said unto them, Nay, but to see the

nakedness of the land ye are come." (verse 12) Of course, they swore the opposite stating they were brothers with the same father, though one brother remained home and the twelfth brother was no more.

Joseph challenges them to prove it. "Send one of you, and let him fetch your brother, and ye shall be kept in prison, that your words may be proved, whether there be any truth in you: or else by the life of Pharaoh surely ye are spies." (verse 16) He imprisons them for three days, then repeats his proposition only in reverse. One man remains bound; the others return home.

The brothers feel terrible, rehashing the great sin they'd committed by selling Joseph; fearful that now Benjamin's life, also, will be taken. Joseph leaves the room and weeps. Why? Because they talked openly in front of him, thinking he did not speak their language, as he used an interpreter.

Now enter the Red Herring. Joseph sends all but one home with food, secretly replacing the silver coins they'd used to make their purchase back in their pouches. He knows they aren't spies. He knows exactly who they are. Yet, he sends them on a quest with no purpose. He forces the central issue off of buying food in Egypt to them proving they aren't spies in order to save their lives. How? By bringing their younger brother, their father's beloved son, Benjamin, back with them to Egypt.

Although they deserved it, the brothers are full of fear, and father Jacob scorns them for not only losing Joseph on their watch, but for now making mention of Benjamin, who would also be taken away from him. All the while, Joseph awaits patiently in

Egypt with a plan to reunite his family and forgive them. Accusing them of spies and sending them on a quest is just a Red Herring sidetrack to buy him time.

So how can you apply this technique to your own writing? The first thing to figure out is why use a Red Herring at all? What's the purpose to pushing the story forward? In the story of Joseph, his motive determines the plot and not the other way around. The Red Herring is a tool to bring his younger brother into his presence (and eventually his father with all their household and belongings). The literary device serves the story.

If you can send the reader on a rabbit trail while maintaining control of your story, the Red Herring will enhance your novel. In *The Da Vinci Code,* Dan Brown leads the reader to believe Bishop Aringarosa is the bad buy, but he serves as the Red Herring to throw the focus off of the real villains. In *Great Expectations,* Charles Dickens vividly leads the reader to believe that Pip's benefactor is the eccentric and wealthy Miss Havisham. We'd bet on it! But she's the Red Herring meant to misdirect the reader's attention away from the escaped convict whom Pip aided, as a small boy, to flee the police. And finally, the Scooby-Doo Mysteries (yep, I went there) base the success of each story on following clues that point the gang toward an innocent, yet likely suspect.

When used well, it works. However, when an author intentionally leads the reader off the trail for the sole purpose of shock value with no furthering or deepening of the plot or character development, the reader will probably get mad.

Are there places in your story where a Red

Herring will enhance your story? Have you added a Red Herring to serve a purpose instead of the plot? What ways can you alter that? Look at some stories that have successfully implemented the Red Herring and those that haven't. Can you list why you feel some worked while others didn't?

For me, when I feel like I've been dragged all over the story world when everything I needed was right in scene one I feel frustrated, unless the author provides a great reason. Books such as *Alice in Wonderland*, *The Wizard of Oz*, and the Underland Chronicles book 6 by Suzanne Collins titled *Gregor and the Curse of the Warmbloods*, utilize the Red Herring in an exceptional fashion. These books take the character on a wonderful adventure in search of answers, be it to find home or find an answer to save home. Only the truth was right in front of them. The Red Herring was the adventure, because the answer was back home on the banks by the river, in Kansas, or in the Kingdom within the Underland. The adventure was necessary for the character to find strength and to grow, something they wouldn't have experienced without the Red Herring adventure. And it worked because it was an organic component of the plot and not something forced into the story to lead the reader astray and teach the characters a lesson.

Chapter Thirty-Eight:

The Darkest Night

The story of Joseph is complex and spans several chapters. As the story goes, it is perfectly crafted to include everything a reader could crave: sex, intrigue, power, deceit, the supernatural, and reconciliation. In Genesis chapter 43, we see an example of the darkest night moment in the story. This is where things are at their worst for our hero, forcing them into the third act and climax, which occurs in Genesis chapter 44 for Joseph.

Joseph sent his brothers home with their money fully restored, telling them to return only with Benjamin, their youngest brother. "And Judah spake unto him, saying, The man did solemnly protest unto us, saying, Ye shall not see my face, except your brother be with you." (verse 3)

This throws Dad into a whirlwind of emotion, berating his children for telling "Joseph" they had a younger brother at all, using the classic line, "You're gonna be the death of me," if anything were to happen to Benjamin, his only remaining son of his beloved Rebecca. But the grain is gone, "And the famine was sore in the land." (verse 1)

The darkest night moment has arrived.

Our characters cannot stay where they are or they will surely die. If they go back to Egypt for food, they must take Benjamin; an odd request without logic, which they assume means he will be killed (and Dad would die of a broken heart in this case). The sacks from the first tip had been filled and their purses reimbursed, so if they returned, the brothers faced death as thieves or spies or both, who knew? There is no good choice. Death awaits at every turn. The ideal darkest night moment falls upon our characters. They are forced to make a choice, the lesser of two evils, knowing their fate is not secure and knowing they are walking into the enemy's camp.

What's Dorothy Gale's darkest night moment in *The Wizard of Oz*? She's reaches the Emerald City, meets the Wizard, and is forced to retrieve the broomstick of the Wicked Witch of the West if she ever wants to return to Kansas. The monkeys come. Dorothy is separated from her friends, but Toto escapes. Then, a crystal ball message from Aunt Em pushes Dorothy over the edge. She agrees to give up the ruby slippers. This means her death. Better to go willing. However, the magic backfires and the witch is angered, unable to remove the ruby slippers as long as Dorothy's alive. The hourglass counts away one piece of sand at a time, the remaining seconds of her life before the witch kills her to take her slippers. Every direction leads to death. Act III has begun.

In *The Hunger Games*, Katniss is betrayed by Peeta, stung by tracker jackers, and then Rue is killed in her arms. She has died on the inside and she realizes she is going to die in the arena. Her darkest night moment has arrived. But then, the commentator explains a change in the rules. Two tributes from the same district can co-win the games. She must find Peeta. Act III has begun.

It's so important that your main character is pressed to this moment where all is lost and defeat (or death) awaits at every turn. This is the place where they can rise at long last to become the hero we, as the reader, have always known they were; able to fulfill their calling.

Have you knocked down your main character enough to remove their options and leave them hopeless? In what ways can you add more elements of defeat and despair? Can you isolate them? Can you bring them to Death's door at every turn? Can you make them desperate?

I would recommend an in-depth study of books and movies you know very well to find and analyze the main character's darkest night moment. What decisions were made? What led them there? What choices remained and what were the consequences of making those choices? By reviewing well-written moments that force characters into the third act, you'll be better able to construct your own story elements and force your character to face their darkest night moment.

And here's a final tip: in this dark place, the character is forced alone with their fatal flaw, the element that paints in the theme. Dorothy sees Aunt

Em and then...just wants to go home, realizes family is more important than anything else; the opposite of her worldview in scene one.

Katniss realizes she can't protect those she loves, helpless from the terrors of the Capital, no matter how hard she tries, and that she needs others to survive; the opposite of her worldview in scene one.

Remember, dig deep and weave those themes and flaws into your character's need to reach their goal. This darkest night moment is where your character's vulnerability is exposed, yet they still choose to fight.

Chapter Thirty-Nine:

The Climax

This is why we read, isn't it?

This is what every story leads to: the climax. We see it in every story, every Bible story, and even in the Bible as a whole with the second coming of Christ in the climax of Revelation. We see it in series, the overarching story line that's resolved once and for all in the final climax in the last book. *Maze Runner. Harry Potter. The Hunger Games.*

In Genesis chapter 44, we are nearing the close of Joseph's story. Let's do a quick recap to really see the impact of the climax. Joseph was the firstborn of Isaac and his favorite wife Rebecca—not the haggard sister. His entire youth, he is treated as the favorite, and no one tries to hide it. Brothers do chores; Joseph is given an expensive robe. And Joseph's a dreamer, but in his dreams, his brothers bow to him. In his dreams, his parents bow to him. Disgusted, the brothers plot to kill Joseph, agreeing instead to sell him into slavery.

Begin Act II. Joseph is bought by Potiphar, and after proving his worth, rises to the highest position in the household. And that doesn't go unnoticed. Potipher's wife tries seducing the sexy, young Hebrew. He refuses more than once, finally running from the cougar embrace, leaving his robe behind. She blows her rape whistle, and he is sent to jail. In prison, Joseph finds favor and is elevated to a position of authority. And then, the dreams. The baker and the cupbearer both dream and Joseph interprets both: they will be released; one will die and one will be restored to his position. "Remember me," Joseph implores. But the cupbearer doesn't. This is our false victory, marking the halfway point in the text.

Three years later, Pharaoh dreams. The cupbearer remembers. Joseph is freed and interprets the dream to becomes head of Egypt under only Pharaoh. He prepares for the famine by storing grain. And it hits. Hard. One by one, people and tribes sell their land for food making Pharaoh the richest man in the world. Enter Joseph's brothers. They don't recognize him. But he knows them. Begin Act III. He toys with them, returning their coins, forcing the retrieval of baby brother Benjamin, hiding treasures in Benjamin's sack—until Joseph can stand it no longer. We have reached the climax in chapter 44.

"And put my cup, the silver cup, in the sack's mouth of the youngest..." (verse 2) Joseph frames Benjamin, only to send out his men later to "find the thief." The brothers swear innocence, even offering unto death the thief, should he be found among them. And the winner is...Benjamin! His life is begged for, and it is agreed that he will lives as a bondservant, though the others must go home. Judah begs for Benjamin's release. He recaps their side of the story, the conversation with Isaac and his impending death, should anything happen to his only "other" son of his beloved Rebeccah. Judah explains, "It shall come to pass, when he seeth that the lad is not with us, that he will die: and thy servants shall bring down the gray hairs of they servant our father with sorrow to the grave." (verse 31) He's really laying it on thick. But the tension is tight.

Will Benjamin live or die?

Will Isaac live or die?

Will Joseph continue to toy with them or will he expose himself?

What will they do when he does reveal his true identity?

As we wait on baited breath, we realize we are at the climax. The story can go either way; good or bad. Life or death. Clean or messy. Happily ever after or not so much.

In *The Hunger Games*, this is the moment when Katniss holds out the Nightlock berries and her and Peeta countdown to their own deaths. The abovementioned questions flit through out minds while we read the book or watch the movie. Will they do it? Will they die? Will we make it? Will something rescue them?

In *The Wizard of Oz*, this is when the hot air balloon lifts and soars of its own accord, leaving Dorothy forever stranded in Oz. Will she stay or go? How? Is the Wizard coming back?

In *The Maze Runner*, we see this when Thomas

plans the jump and everyone knows it will kill them too. Will they make it? Will they live? What's on the other side of that wall? Is it worse than what they're leaving? How many will die?

As you reach your story's climax, don't rush things. Give the reader that sense of hopelessness, those insurmountable odds, and no way out. Get them to the point where they need a miracle, and then rush the reader through the fear, the unknown, the chaos you've created until, breathless, we all reach the other side.

Have you made your climax too weak? What other obstacles could you add in leading up to it? Have you made things too easy for your characters? Where can you amp up the tension and the stakes to create a more impactful climax?

By studying other stories, you will notice those places just before the climax where you are uncertain if the hero will make it or not. Learn from them. Begin to build in those same moments that will cause your reader to wonder and fear the same things.

Chapter Forty:

It's never too late

As an author your task is to give your reader enough information to reveal the story as you go, and nothing more. That doesn't mean you withhold valuable plot or character development to create a surprise ending. But it does mean that sometimes a story or character may be presented in one light while all the while something entirely different is going on. The best example of this technique is the movie *The Sixth Sense* by M. Night Shyamalan. If you don't know it, stop reading this book and go watch that film—though you'll have to watch a second time after you get to the end. Trust me. In storytelling, it's never too late for a character reveal that shifts the plot. In fact, it's why we read. But this shift has to serve the story, not added in for effect. Otherwise, we won't be happy readers.

When Darth Vader is revealed as Luke's father and Leah's sister in *The Empire Strikes Back*, it changes everything; so much so that the series goes back to the beginning in the 2000s to show Vader's decline from Anakin Skywalker to the ruthless villain just before the birth of his twins. In the Harry Potter franchise, we are flabbergasted when Dumbledore reveals that he knew all along that Harry would have to die one day to defeat Voldemort, and Dumbledore's willingness to sacrifice his "son" for the greater good. Then, we discover how Snape shares not only a love for Harry's mother, but a sacrificial promise to care for and protect Harry from the shadows. It's completely unexpected and so powerful that it shifts our perspective of these characters forever. Now *that's* good storytelling!

In Genesis chapter 45, Joseph faces his brothers as the leader of Egypt. What do they do? They bow, of course, fulfilling prophetic dreams. His heart can stand it no longer. "Then Joseph could not refrain himself before all them that stood by him; and he cried, caused every man to go out from him. And there stood no man with him, while Joseph made himself known unto his brethren." (verse 1)

After all they've done to him and all he's put them through, the truth is finally revealed. Their response? They were troubled at his presence. (verse 3) You'd think they'd be excited, relieved, grateful even. But instead, Joseph must explain how their decision to sell him into slavery enabled him to be in that place, in that moment, in order to store food to keep them alive during the famine and preserve the continuation of his family line. Wow. That's some serious vision. "And God sent me before you to preserve you a posterity in the earth, and to save your lives by a great deliverance." (verse 7)

Joseph is a big picture kinda guy. He always has been. He doesn't see any of those horrible things that happened to him as mistakes or bad choices, nor does he harbor bitterness or unforgiveness toward any of those who caused it. But it's hard for everyone to see life that way.

In time, all of Egypt learns that Joseph's brothers have arrived and the whole land celebrates. The brothers are instructed to go home, gather their families and their father, and return to Egypt, for the famine was only halfway through its cycle. "Also regard not your stuff; for the good of all the land of Egypt is yours." (verse 20) Not such a bad reunion for these brothers who once plotted kill Joseph, who now had the authority to kill them.

The brothers were given provisions, wagons, clothing, and coin to head home and get their families. When they told their father that Joseph was alive and the governor of Egypt, "his heart fainted for he believed them not." (verse 26) But when he saw all the animals, provisions, carts, and clothing bearing Pharaoh's insignia, he believed and said, "It is enough; Joseph my son is yet alive: I will go and see him before I die." (verse 28)

It's never too late.

In your story, have you built up to character and plot twists that surprise the reader? Do these moments happen organically from the plot or have you developed a plot to serve the surprise? It's very important that you don't write a whole story to serve a "Wow!" moment at the end. That's a mistake many writers fall into and the story can tend to read like a Scooby-Doo Mystery. Build in moments that act as clues for the steadfast reader, but don't appear so obvious that they give themselves away. Then, when your story leads to the big reveal, your reader will think back upon the breadcrumbs you've scattered along the way and feel satisfied knowing they were aware; yet surprised because they didn't fully connect the dots.

There's nothing worse than figuring out a whole story halfway through because the author planted obvious clues to push the story toward a planned, surprise ending. Instead, use your story to move the plot and find those threads you've already created. Weave them together to produce that surprise ending and no one will see it coming, not even you! Just remember, it's never too late.

Chapter Forty-One:

Reconciliation

In fiction, as in life, humans seek reconciliation, peace, and harmony. That doesn't mean we are always willing or able to achieve it, but no one likes uneasiness, discomfort, turmoil, or chaos. Mankind's just not built that way. After everything that's happened with his family, in Genesis 46, Jacob is about to find a reconciliation he never believed possible. His son was dead; his other son kept prisoner. Now he's told both are alive and well. Joseph is ruling Egypt with baby brother Benjamin safely by his side in the palace.

"And Jacob rose up from Beer-sheba: and the sons of Israel carried Jacob their father, and their little ones, and their wives, in the wagons which Pharaoh had sent to carry him." (verse 5)

He's moving up in the world just in time for retirement! So are his children, and their families, and the whole lot of them. God had made a promise to

Abraham that he would be the father of a great nation, and he reminds Jacob in this moment that he is keeping that promise. How? By placing Joseph in charge of Egypt and the family caravanning to be with him. It's pretty amazing how what appeared to be a grievous act by the brothers—to kill Joseph—led to the fulfillment of God's promise; Joseph, savior of the world. Talk about good plotting! We have so much to learn from Joseph's story about the perfection of storytelling, plotting, foreshadowing, and character development. Can you tell it's my favorite?

Verses 8-25 account for each brother's family— the tribes—taking their journey to include 66 people altogether. My thoughts for the inclusion of this information is to compare it later to the number of Hebrew slaves that accumulate in Egypt nearly 400 years later. The back-story to foreshadow the great population of God's promised nation.

Here's the moment we've been waiting for. the caravan approaches Goshen, having sent Judah ahead to inform Joseph of their arrival. I can visualize the expanse of desert, with mountains climbing out of sight on either side, and a setting sun burning crimson. Two groups approach: the Pharaoh's coaches carrying Joseph's family, and Joseph in his royal chariot. The horses churn up dust; the music fades. Joseph rushes into his father's embrace as a man, and they weep, neither one ever believing this day would come.

"And Israel (Jacob) said unto Joseph, Now let me die, since I have seen thy face, because thou art yet alive." (verse 30)

Reconciliation. It's a beautiful thing.

We see it in great stories. *A Christmas Carol.*

The Wizard of Oz. It's A Wonderful Life. We witness the act within stories, like when Frodo and Sam make amends. In *How the Grinch Stole Christmas,* when the Whos and the Grinch reconcile and forgive. In *The Phantom Tollbooth,* Milo reconciles two kingdoms: Digitopolis (numbers) and Dictionopolis (words).

Building a scene where characters or kingdoms reconcile is no easy task. The further apart they grow and the least likely the possibility for future interaction, the greater the end result. Time doesn't heal all wounds. Sometimes, they fester.

We love Ebenezer Scrooge, not because he is fair to his employees, charitable with his great excess of wealth, or cordial at family dinners. Those are expected social norms. What pulls at our heartstrings is watching him behave in this manner after we saw what a jerk he was, not only in the present, but also in the past and future. His wide reaching transformation makes the reconciliation more dramatic. There is so much opposition between who he was and who he becomes in the end. It is this deep, vast cavern of difference that makes us love this story nearly 200 years later.

Have you built in drama and hurts that are left unaddressed? Has time and distance compounded these feelings to make the drama larger than it really is? Have you presented the appearance of no possible solutions? Good. You've set up the perfect storm for a dynamic reconciliation.

Chapter Forty-Two:

Setting Up the Sequel

One great thing about being a writer is leaving bread trails that lead to book two. The first story should stand alone, like the story of Joseph in Egypt, but indications and unanswered problems can hang out like threads for you to begin book two.

In Genesis 47, Joseph's story with his family has reached a close. His early visions have come to pass with the stars, moon, and sun, all bowing before him in the physical form of his brothers, mother, and father bowing before him as the sub-ruler of Egypt. We have reached the story's climax. Enter the falling action. But woven within the seams is the setup for the next epic story: Moses and the slaves of Egypt.

"And Pharaoh spake unto Joseph, saying, Thy father and thy brethren are come unto thee:" (verse 5). The family is now together in Egypt. Why? To fulfill God's promise long ago to Abraham that he would father a great nation. How can this happen if all of his offspring perish in the famine?

And the famine rages on. Joseph's family (and God's promise) lay just outside its deadly grasp. "And Joseph nourished his father, and his brethren, and all his father's household, with bread according to their families." (verse 12)

But things are about to grow worse.

Back in Genesis 15:13, there is a prediction that the children of Israel would be strangers in a strange land and enter into slave bondage for 400 years, afflicted as servants, until the time when God would set them free. This moment here in Genesis 47 is the precursor for that event. Joseph has saved enough grain to feed his people and the entire known world. As the famine progresses, the people spend their last coins, making Egypt the only nation with gold. "And Joseph said, Give your cattle; and I will give you for cattle if money fail." (verse 16) And they do. But it isn't enough.

The famine continues, so the people give up their land, making Egypt the richest, most powerful nation in the world. The people are given seed to farm, with the agreement that 1/5 of their harvest belongs to the Pharaoh. They comply; they survive.

In this manner, we have a great setup for book two: the story of Moses. We have a land more powerful than the rest with the Israelites taking a key role and place within the city gates to grow and multiply, living off the best land with the most lenient requirements to Pharaoh. In several hundred years, however, the new Pharaoh knows them not and feels threatened by their numbers.

Setting up the sequel requires a clear resolution

of the story problem presented in book one, while leaving some details unresolved to continue the overarching story problem that connects the books in a series. *Divergent, The Hunger Games, Maze Runner,* and *Harry Potter*, each demonstrate the careful balance of closing the story problem with a clear resolution while keeping a larger problem unsolved until the final book in the series.

If you are planning a sequel, did you end your first book with a satisfying close? Did you solve the current story problem or did you end on a cliffhanger to secure book two? If book one requires book two to be complete, you haven't done your job as an author and have broken the unspoken contract with your reader. Your job is to present and resolve a problem within the book's pages. Not every problem, but that particular book's problem. Instead, you have strung the reader along for 300 or so pages only to smack a big "To Be Continued" in their faces.

The only time you can pull this off is the transition between book two and book three, or the second to last book and the last book if your series is greater than a trilogy. Your reader is invested by that point. Plus book two should end on a hopeless note. You almost require a book three after book two when it ends low. *The Empire Strikes Back. Catching Fire. The Scorch Trials.* These three series have an "all is lost" ending to book (or movie) two that continues into book (or movie) three to close the series. Your reader is invested by the end of book two and willing to accept your "To Be Continued" sign.

As an example, *The Hunger Games* trilogy didn't need a book two or three. We had a clear close and were satisfied with the ending. But at the end of book two, we were left on a cliffhanger and had to continue to book three if we wanted to know how the overall story ended. The formula is executed perfectly by Suzanne Collins.

The same can be true of the *Back to the Future* trilogy, which literally types "To Be Continued" before the ending credits of the movie. The break at the end of book two requires you to move into the third film, because Marty McFly is stuck in 1955 and Doc Brown is somewhere in the old West. The chase is on.

Look for ways to clearly close book one while leaving subtle hints that book two and three are right around the corner, should you choose to continue to create new problems for the characters and worlds you've created as an author.

Chapter Forty-Three:

Falling Action

Genesis 48 reminds me of the final twenty minutes of *The Lord of the Rings: The Return of the King*. The ring has been destroyed, Middle Earth has won, and the arduous journey is over. Frodo awakens to his friends from the Shire, and there is fellowship, laughter, and love.

But the story doesn't stop here.

The falling action starts. We head back to the Shire, we talk with Bilbo, he releases his first book, and goes essentially on a book tour. Sam asks out the Hobbit woman of his dreams, they marry, and everyone lives happily ever after, even Frodo, whose price for magic is to leave the Shire he loved so much, forever.

I say every time I see this extended falling action that it could have been stretched into an entire movie.

Falling action, like the introduction, should be

just long enough to close the loose ends of the story. Once the climax peaks, your reader has received the satisfaction they've been waiting for. They don't necessarily want to stick around too much longer. And they definitely don't want to feel like they're stuck turning pages. A great meal with perfect ambiance, food, and service, can be ruined if it takes too long to get the bill after dessert.

This is what happens in Genesis chapter 48. Joseph reveals himself to his brothers. He forgives them. They move with Dad to Egypt. Jacob has reunited with his thought-to-be-dead favorite son who happens to pretty much rule Egypt. They are rescued from death by famine. The story climax has passed. The reader feels satisfied.

But then, "And it came to pass after these things, that one told Joseph, Behold, thy father is sick: and he took with him his two sons, Manasseh and Ephraim." (verse 1)

So the story isn't quite over. Jacob is dying. And when Joseph enters to say good-bye, Jacob goes through this long history of events leading to the present (my *Lord of the Rings* moment) to include the death of his wife, her burial, and, of course, God's promise of a great nation; the story thread in the Bible from Abraham to Moses.

Then, he takes Joseph's sons to bless them and Joseph positions them with his firstborn closest to Jacob's right hand (the best blessing) and his second closest to his left hand. The father always blessed the firstborn with his right hand. Well, Jacob just crosses his hand, positioning his right hand over the youngest and giving him the blessing, even after Joseph tries to literally move Dad's hand to the firstborn.

"And his (Joseph's) father refused, and said, I know it, my son, I know it: he shall also become a people, and he also shall be great: but truly his younger brother shall be greater than he, and his seed shall become a multitude of nations." (verse 19)

Oh, the irony!

Joseph, the favorite, the eleventh born of his father, is "displeased" by his father's favoritism with Manasseh and Ephraim. It's classic, really. And Jacob, his father, was the favorite of his mother, Rebecca, who tricked his father, Isaac, into giving him his older brother, Esau's, blessing. And the curse spins on and on.

As a writer, you must be careful not to provide too much falling action or not enough. When a story ends too soon, it can feel rushed and leave the reader with unanswered questions. When it' too long, it can be frustrating. In either case, a wonderful novel can leave a bad taste in your reader's mouth if you don't craft a well-balanced falling action and ending.

And bad taste means bad reviews, and even losing readers.

Have you tried cramming an entire book into your falling action? How much of that information is for you, the writer, verses how much of it is necessary for your reader to answer story questions? Do you have another book in the falling action that you can use for a sequel or series? If not, would the information be better served as an epilogue?

The other choice is to let the information sit in the "bonus material" section, like on a DVD, where you can review behind the scenes footage, see hilarious outtakes, or even alternate endings. The extended falling action can be shaved down to bare bones, and the rest can be slowly trickled out on social media sites to build buzz.

Chapter Forty-Four:

Beyond the Main Character

"And Jacob called unto his sons, and said, Gather yourselves together, that I may tell you that which shall befall you in the last days." (Genesis 49:1)

Wow! What an opening line.

What struck me is how Jacob is sharing a story with his family about events yet to come, long after they are all gone, but as a direct result of the experiences in their own story. He then spends the next twenty-eight verses individually describing and blessing his children, which got me thinking: everyone has a story.

Even if it's not the main story, every character in your book has a story. Whether or not the reader ever learns about it, every character in your book has their own past, present, and future.

Some stories seem honorable: "Reuben, thou art my firstborn, my might, and the beginning of my strength, the excellency of dignity, and the excellency of power: (verse 3) Those stories sometimes have unhappy endings: "Unstable as water, thou shalt not excel; because thou wentest up to thy father's bed; then defiledst thou it: he went up to my couch." (verse 4)

Can you imagine this guy's demeanor changing from puffed out and boastful to hunched over and broken as his father spoke those words over him? Jacob didn't have very nice things to say about Simeon or Levi either in verses 5-7. The stories for Zebulon (verse 13) and Naphtali (verse 21) are neutral. And the great blessings are bestowed upon the remaining brothers: Judah Issachar, Dan, Gad, Joseph, and Benjamin. Now of these men, Joseph has remained the main character of this story so far. But what about Judah? Of all those names, his rings a bell: the Lion of Judah. His story will lead to the birth of the Messiah.

Which leads me to the second point when thinking beyond main characters, and this is the spin off series. We've seen it before. *The Chronicles of Riddick* spun off of *Pitch Black* because the character of Riddick was so interesting that audiences needed to know his story. The movie *Creed* is the continuation of Rocky's story through the life of his friend Apollo Creed's son, who is now becoming a fighter. *Fantastic Beasts and Where to Find Them* is a spin off from the wizarding world of *Harry Potter*. Not a sequel, not a prequel, but a continuation of the world in a new universe. We see similar stories appearing in the *Star Wars* universe and Tolkien's worlds.

In Genesis 50, Jacob is dead. His brothers once again transpire against Joseph, deciding that now that his father is gone, Joseph will make them pay for what they did to him all those years ago. They still don't even get the story of which they were a part. But Joseph utters one of my favorite verses in Genesis 50:20: "But as for you, ye thought evil against me; but God meant it unto good, to bring to pass, as it is this day, to save much people alive."

God has his own spin off story in mind: the story of Moses, and eventually the story of Jesus. "And Joseph took an oath of the children of Israel, saying, God will surely visit you, and ye shall carry up my bones from here." (verse 25)

And his story ends.

Have you created complex supporting characters with their own stories, goals, motivations, and fears? Or are they flat and uninteresting, simply there to fill in and aid the hero on their journey? Do they prompt the reader to want to know more? How can you build supporting characters strong enough to support their own story while still knowing their place in the story at hand?

What about world building? Have you created a milieu so incredible that the reader craves more stories set within its boundaries? Through balance, you can create believable worlds and characters that your reader will love so much that they insist you share more once they read The End.

Author's Note

The lessons and conclusions in this book are my own. They are based off my opinions and inspiration as I read each chapter of the book of Genesis, watched movies or television shows, and read books. I'm certain that you gleaned additional concepts and ideas as you read along and I would love to hear those thoughts.

As an author, I love interacting with people who read my books. Your thoughts and opinions matter, and knowing that I've touched you through my words, or more importantly in the case of this book through His Word, is the reason I do what I do. Please feel free to comment through my website's online form at awriterforlife.com. Once there, you can link to my social media sites and follow my SELL MORE BOOKS! newsletter.

I am so blessed to spend each day doing what I love, and to share what I've learned on my journey with other authors. I am available for coaching, editing, and marketing services or to speak to your writing group, Bible Study group, or to teach at your conference. It's what I do.

In closing, I leave you with Numbers 6:24-26 "May the Lord Bless you and keep you. May the Lord make his face shine upon you and be gracious to you. May the Lord lift up his countenance upon you and give you peace."

Happy Writing!

Works Cited & Websites

Harry Potter Series
Lord of the Rings Trilogy
Pinocchio
Legend
Percy Jackson Series
Robin Hood
The Matrix
X-Men
Superman
It's A Wonderful Life
Hunger Games Trilogy
The Wizard of Oz
Realtruth.org
Indiana Jones Franchise
Journey to the Center of the Earth
The Time Machine
Gone With the Wind
The Fault of Our Stars
50 Shades of Gray

Jerry Maguire
Ender's Game
The Chronicles of Narnia
Star Wars Franchise
Holes
The Lemonade War
Cinder
Beezus and Ramona
Batman
Back to the Future Trilogy
On Writing
Carrie
Orson Buggy's Big Fang Theory
Lord of the Flies
Goldilocks and the Three Bears
Divergent
Rita Hayworth and the

Shawshank
Redemption
The Life of Pi
The Hobbit
300
Rambo
Shrek
Monk
Dumbo
Looper
Pitch Black
Behindthenames.com
Shecknows.com
Disney
Aladdin
The Lion King
The Princess and the
Frog
Invasion of the Body
Snatchers
The Lottery
Lynnwood
Thinner
The Tell-Tale Heart
The Monkey's Paw
A Christmas Carol
The Maze Runner
Gregor the Overlander
Spiderman
Cinderella
The Man in the Iron
Mask
Biblestudytool.com

Twilight
Vocabulary.com
Supernatural
Catching Fire
Revenge of the Sith
Snow White
Romeo and Juliet
The Geneva Project
Breaking Dawn
The Da Vinci Code
Great Expectations
Scooby-Doo Mysteries
The Underland
Chronicles
Gregor and the Curse of
the Warmbloods
The Sixth Sense
How the Grinch Stole
Christmas
The Phantom Tollbooth
The Chronicles of
Riddick
Greed
Fantastic Beasts and
Where to Find Them
Dreadlands
Clifton Chase and the
Arrow of Light
The Dredge

If you enjoyed this book, please take a moment to review it on Amazon for other readers to discover it.

Become a fan

 @awriterforlifecoach   @awriterforlife

Available for coaching, marketing, & speaking.
Visit awriterforlife.com for dates.

Jaimie Engle has written professionally since 2003 with more than 100 publications in journals and e-mags throughout the world. In 2013, she published her first middle-grade novel *Clifton Chase and the Arrow of Light* an anti-bullying fantasy adventure awarded a B.R.A.G. Medallion in 2015, and *The Dredge* in 2014, which won the L. Ron Hubbard's Writers of the Future Award. Engle is a regular conference speaker with the Space Coast Writer's Guild, Eastern Florida State College, the Orange County & Brevard County Library Systems, and the Society of Children Book Writer's & Illustrators. She speaks regularly to students in Lake and Brevard County, Florida. Engle offers a coaching & editing service for aspiring writers at www.awriterforlife.com. Learn more about her books at www.jmebooks.com.

Made in the USA
Charleston, SC
27 February 2017